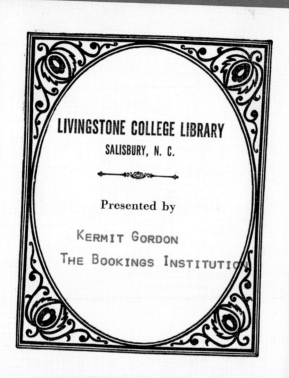

BREAD UPON THE WATERS
Federal Aids to the Maritime Industries

GERALD R. JANTSCHER

Since the Second World War more than $10 billion of direct federal assistance has been pumped into American shipping and shipbuilding industries, and yet this is only part of the story. In addition to operating and construction subsidies paid to them directly, the U. S. maritime industries receive a variety of other benefits. Much government business is set aside for them by statute. A substantial portion of shipping profits is sheltered from income taxes. And in some markets both industries are protected from foreign competition.

American taxpayers and consumers foot this bill; what do they get in return? Economic advantages? Greater national security? A mobile showcase promoting American ability, technology, and ingenuity in all parts of the world?

The author examines the major forms of aid to the maritime industries, the reasons for their existence, and what they cost the public. First, he analyzes the operating and construction subsidies, the cabotage laws governing the nation's domestic oceanborne commerce, and the cargo preference laws, which require half or more of "government-impelled cargo" (military supplies and personnel, food for peace shipments, and foreign aid) to be shipped in U. S.-built and U. S.-registered vessels. He reviews the tax subsidies to the maritime industries that constitute a form of public assistance available to no other industry. Then he evaluates the effect of these various forms of subsidy on the national economy, national security, and public well-being.

His conclusion: the only rationale for maritime subsidies that stands scrutiny on the facts available is the national security argument—ships flying the American flag may be needed in times of crisis. But he also concludes that if this *is* the objective of maritime subsidies, then the program of aid is wrongly focused and wrongly administered.

Gerald R. Jantscher is a member of the staff of the Brookings Economic Studies program and author of another Brookings book, *Trusts and Estate Taxation* (1967).

Studies in the Regulation of Economic Activity
TITLES PUBLISHED

Studies in the Regulation of Economic Activity

Bread upon the Waters: Federal Aids to the Maritime Industries

GERALD R. JANTSCHER

The Brookings Institution / *Washington, D.C.*

Library of Congress Cataloging in Publication Data:
Jantscher, Gerald R
  Bread upon the waters.

  (Studies in the regulation of economic activity)
  Includes bibliographical references.
    1. Merchant marine—United States. 2. Shipping—
United States. 3. Subsidies—United States. I. Brook-
ings Institution, Washington, D.C. II. Title.
III. Series.
HE741.J35   387.5′1   75-1067
ISBN 0-8157-4574-5

9 8 7 6 5 4 3 2 1

THE BROOKINGS INSTITUTION is an independent organization devoted to nonpartisan research, education, and publication in economics, government, foreign policy, and the social sciences generally. Its principal purposes are to aid in the development of sound public policies and to promote public understanding of issues of national importance.

The Institution was founded on December 8, 1927, to merge the activities of the Institute for Government Research, founded in 1916, the Institute of Economics, founded in 1922, and the Robert Brookings Graduate School of Economics and Government, founded in 1924.

The Board of Trustees is responsible for the general administration of the Institution, while the immediate direction of the policies, program, and staff is vested in the President, assisted by an advisory committee of the officers and staff. The by-laws of the Institution state, "It is the function of the Trustees to make possible the conduct of scientific research, and publication, under the most favorable conditions, and to safeguard the independence of the research staff in the pursuit of their studies and in the publication of the results of such studies. It is not a part of their function to determine, control, or influence the conduct of particular investigations or the conclusions reached."

The President bears final responsibility for the decision to publish a manuscript as a Brookings book or staff paper. In reaching his judgment on the competence, accuracy, and objectivity of each study, the President is advised by the director of the appropriate research program and weighs the views of a panel of expert outside readers who report to him in confidence on the quality of the work. Publication of a work signifies that it is deemed to be a competent treatment worthy of public consideration; such publication does not imply endorsement of conclusions or recommendations contained in the study.

The Institution maintains its position of neutrality on issues of public policy in order to safeguard the intellectual freedom of the staff. Hence interpretations or conclusions in Brookings publications should be understood to be solely those of the author or authors and should not be attributed to the Institution, to its trustees, officers, or other staff members, or to the organizations that support its research.

Foreword

No INDUSTRY in the United States has a longer history of aid from the federal government than the ship-operating and shipbuilding industries. Assistance began with the second act of the First Congress, passed soon after George Washington was inaugurated, and has continued ever since. Today the maritime industries are the beneficiaries of an extensive array of federal aids. Operating and construction subsidies are paid to them directly, and much government business is reserved to them by statute. A large part of shipping profits can be sheltered from income taxation. In some private markets both industries are protected by law from foreign competition.

The cost of these aids, paid by taxpayers and consumers, is sizable. Since the Second World War the maritime industries have received assistance costing more than $10 billion. The operating and construction subsidies currently amount to over $400 million a year, and other aids cost millions more. A large shipbuilding program for the United States merchant marine that began in 1971 ensures that costs will remain high for years to come.

In this study Gerald R. Jantscher describes the major aids to the maritime industries, examines their rationale, and presents estimates of their cost. Proponents tend to stress the beneficial effects of the assistance program on employment, output, and public revenue and its improvement of the nation's balance of payments, but Jantscher finds these effects largely illusory or questionable. He concludes that maritime aids can only be justified by the contribution they make to the nation's security, but adds that by this criterion the current assistance program is highly defective because it is primarily oriented toward commercial objectives rather than defense requirements. He believes that the national security argument for maritime aids should be reconsidered and that if assistance is warranted the program should be designed to serve defense needs explicitly.

The author is a member of the staff of the Economic Studies program of the Brookings Institution. For wise counsel and cordial assistance, he wishes to thank Barry M. Blechman, Walter J. Chilman, Samuel A. Lawrence, James R. McCaul, Ransford W. Palmer, Walter S. Salant, Charles L. Schultze, John P. Tebeau, Ralph L. Trisko, and many other persons too numerous to list in the U.S. Maritime Administration, Agency for International Development, Military Sealift Command, U.S. Department of the Treasury, and other federal offices and private organizations. The author is also indebted to Barrington K. Brown and Evelyn P. Fisher for carefully checking figures and citations, Margaret Markley and Valerie J. Harris for secretarial help, Barbara P. Haskins for editing the manuscript, and Florence Robinson for preparing the index.

This book is the twelfth of the Brookings series of Studies in the Regulation of Economic Activity. The series presents the findings of a program of research on public policies toward business. The program is supported by a grant from the Ford Foundation and is directed by Joseph A. Pechman, director of the Brookings Economic Studies program, and Roger G. Noll, professor of economics at the California Institute of Technology and a former Brookings senior fellow. Some of the descriptive material in this volume previously appeared in *The Economics of Federal Subsidy Programs,* a compendium of papers published by the Joint Economic Committee of Congress.

The views expressed in this book are those of the author and should not be ascribed to those whose assistance is acknowledged above, or to the trustees, officers, or other staff members of the Brookings Institution or the Ford Foundation.

KERMIT GORDON
President

December 1974
Washington, D.C.

Contents

Tables

BREAD UPON THE WATERS

Federal Aids to the Maritime Industries

GERALD R. JANTSCHER

Studies in the Regulation of Economic Activity
THE BROOKINGS INSTITUTION

Bread upon the Waters

CHAPTER ONE

Introduction

THERE ARE few industries in the United States in whose affairs the federal government has played so active a role as the merchant shipping industry. Nearly every aspect of the industry's operations is affected by some public measure or action that was expressly designed with shipping in mind. An entire title of the United States Code contains nothing but federal laws relating to shipping—and other relevant laws appear elsewhere. International treaties and conventions also constrain the industry's behavior.

The interest that the government takes in the nation's merchant marine is as old as the United States. The second and third acts of the First Congress established lower duties on certain imports when carried in the ships of U.S. citizens than when carried in the ships of foreigners and imposed higher tonnage duties on foreign vessels entering U.S. ports than on U.S. vessels. Both were early attempts to promote a national fleet. The First Congress also enacted other statutes affecting shipping, such as measures establishing a registry system for vessels and regulating coastal shipping.

Today service, regulation, and promotion are the three broad areas of government involvement in the shipping industry. The government serves not only the U.S. merchant marine but also ships of other nations in diverse ways: by erecting and maintaining navigational aids, for example, or keeping channels free from obstruction and participating in the International Ice Patrol. It regulates the U.S. maritime industry through such vehicles as the sizable body of law developed to control working conditions aboard U.S. vessels and the Interstate Commerce and Federal Maritime Commissions, which approve freight rates.

The government's third role—as promoter of the national maritime industries—is the subject of this book. The term "maritime industries" is used here to mean the U.S. shipping and shipbuilding industries. In general the federal government is much less involved in the affairs of the shipbuilding industry than in those of shipping. The shipbuilding industry receives no special services from the government, nor is it subject to special regulation. But the government does promote the industry's welfare by measures designed to stimulate sales. These promotional efforts were initiated as long ago as those the government exerts on behalf of shipping. The same early laws that discriminated in favor of American-owned vessels by means of preferential import and tonnage duties also favored ships built in the United States. Although it would be possible to study government aids to the two industries separately, they are in practice so intertwined that to divide them in this manner would be artificial. And so this book is a study of federal aids to both U.S. industries, with somewhat more emphasis on shipping than shipbuilding.

Diversity of Federal Aids

The federal government promotes the U.S. maritime industries primarily by administering an extensive program of maritime aids. The aids are given in a multiplicity of forms, constituting an assistance program of unrivaled diversity. No other federal program exemplifies so many distinct forms of subsidy. Some are given directly, such as the operating differential and construction differential subsidies. Some are given indirectly, in payments the government makes for the services it buys. Others are administered through the tax system, or by laws protecting producers from foreign competition. The aggregate value of all this assistance is sizable and apparently growing larger.

The purpose of this book is to describe the principal aids that these industries receive, estimate their cost to the U.S. public, and evaluate the reasons that are commonly offered to justify this assistance. It would be impossible in a brief study such as this to fully describe all public aids to the maritime industries. They are too numerous and too varied. Accordingly only the most important are discussed here.[1]

The U.S. shipping industry includes a large inland waterways fleet of towboats and barges and a Great Lakes fleet consisting chiefly of ore and

---

1. For example, this book does not cover the insurance programs that the government operates for the benefit of shipowners, which enable them to procure mortgage insurance and war risk insurance that would otherwise be either unobtainable or obtainable only at a prohibitive price. Nor does it deal with federally sponsored training and health programs. The government supports a federal merchant marine academy that trains officers for the industry, and it makes payments to several similar schools operated by states. Merchant seamen may also obtain health care at a number of hospitals around the country that are operated for their benefit by the U.S. Public Health Service. These and other programs that may properly be called maritime aids are beyond the scope of this study, which is limited to the primary forms of federal assistance.

coal carriers. Both are excluded from the scope of this study. The part of the shipping industry of primary concern here is the ocean shipping fleet. Its problems are quite different from those of inland operators, and the government's response to them has been different. It is true that the federal government has promoted inland shipping for nearly as long as it has promoted ocean shipping, but by other methods and for other reasons. The familiar federal aids that come to mind when "maritime subsidies" are mentioned were fashioned for the oceangoing fleet and were only recently extended to other parts of the industry.[2]

Federal aids to the maritime industries are commonly known as maritime subsidies. Subsidy, however, is a technical term for a particular kind of money transfer from the public to the private sector. The maritime industries receive assistance in many forms, some of which are far from being subsidies in the strict sense of the term. And so the word is used sparingly in this book, except where warranted.

This book has much to say about U.S. flag vessels—vessels of the U.S. merchant marine. The term refers to ships registered under the laws of the United States and privileged to fly the American flag. All oceangoing ships must have some nationality in order to claim the protection of international law. Until this century vessels were normally registered under the national flags of their owners. Especially since the Second World War, however, it has become common for shipowners of one nationality—a corporation established under the laws of the United Kingdom, for example—to register their ships under another flag, that of Liberia being a popular choice. Many U.S. shipowners have followed this practice to avoid the obligations imposed on them by U.S. law in return for U.S. registry.[3] Although owned by U.S. citizens, such ships are not U.S. flag vessels.

2. The inland shipping industry is thriving and is now much larger than the U.S. ocean shipping industry. There is no question that the government has fostered its growth by such direct and indirect measures as improving waterways and refusing to permit railroads to lower their rates in order to compete more vigorously with inland operators. Cabotage laws protect the Great Lakes fleet from Canadian competition for the carriage of cargoes between American ports. The Great Lakes fleet also receives navigational services from the government and recently became eligible for some of the same promotional aids that are given to the deepsea industry.

3. The chief obligation is that 75 percent of the ship's crew and all of its officers must be U.S. citizens. This requirement greatly increases the ship's operating costs. However, there are also other reasons why owners prefer registry under a foreign flag. For further discussion of this point, see Boleslaw Adam Boczek, *Flags of Convenience: An International Legal Study* (Harvard University Press, 1962), chap. 2, and the references cited there.

Recent History of the Shipping Industry

The oceangoing U.S. merchant marine has changed both in size and function several times during this century. Before the First World War only a small U.S. fleet traded overseas, and the United States depended heavily on the fleets of other nations to carry its foreign commerce. A much larger U.S. fleet served the domestic trades, sailing along the nation's coasts, between the coasts, and between the mainland and distant territories and possessions. After entering the war the United States embarked on a major program of ship construction. The nation's shipyards succeeded in delivering a large number of new vessels, but most of them only after the war was over. Faced with the problem of what to do with so much excess tonnage, the government reacted by attempting to transfer many of the ships to private ownership. The roots of the current subsidy program can be traced to these years when the government became more entangled in shipping affairs than it had ever been before.

The United States possessed a large, up-to-date fleet in the early twenties; but few new vessels were added thereafter. By the middle of the 1930s many observers of maritime affairs were concerned that the U.S. merchant marine would soon become gravely handicapped in its competition with ships of other nations as many of the vessels built during the war approached the end of their useful lives. It was in part the aging of the fleet that spurred Congress to enact a program of construction aids in 1936, which has continued ever since and is today an important part of the maritime assistance program.

The Second World War had of course a devastating effect on the merchant fleets of all nations. Millions of tons of shipping were sunk. The fleets of the Axis powers were destroyed, while those of the Allies suffered heavy losses. But thanks to an impressive wartime shipbuilding program, the United States actually quadrupled the size of its merchant marine between 1941 and 1945 and emerged from the war owning the largest fleet that the world had ever seen.[4]

4. On September 1, 1939, the U.S. fleet was the second largest in the world, with 13.9 percent of the gross registered tonnage of all the world's oceangoing commercial steam and motor ships of 1,000 gross tons and over. Only the fleet of the United Kingdom was larger, with nearly twice the tonnage of the American fleet. On December 31, 1946, the U.S. fleet contained 50.6 percent of the world's tonnage. (Data are from *Merchant Fleets of the World: Oceangoing Steam and Motor Ships of 1,000 Gross Tons and Over*, published semiannually by the U.S. Maritime Administration.)

The period just after the war is still fondly remembered by many industry leaders as the heyday of American maritime supremacy, when the U.S. merchant marine carried a large part of the world's commerce and a much larger share of U.S. exports and imports than it had since the earliest years of the republic. Of course these halcyon days could not last. The circumstances were abnormal. The great prewar maritime nations were bound to rebuild their merchant fleets after they had recovered from the war's destruction. The United States aided their recovery with its large-scale foreign aid programs and directly assisted in the rebuilding of their fleets by selling abroad at bargain prices many of the vessels that had been built during the war. More than one thousand government-owned merchant vessels were sold to foreign nationals between 1946 and 1948, out of a total of more than four thousand that the government decided were surplus to its needs.[5]

At the same time, U.S. citizens were also given the opportunity to buy government-owned vessels, and many did. They bought 746 ships under authority of the Merchant Ship Sales Act of 1946 at prices even lower than those that foreign buyers paid.[6] U.S. buyers were also given first pick of the available ships. In this manner the privately owned U.S. merchant marine was considerably expanded after the war. Most of the unsold government-owned ships were laid up and placed in the National Defense Reserve Fleet.[7]

It was downhill thereafter for the U.S. merchant fleet until the early 1970s. The fleet steadily contracted until in 1970 it was only the fifth, sixth, or seventh largest in the world, depending on the measure of size used. Many of the same warbuilt vessels were still in service—only now the ships were obsolete and uneconomical, destined soon for the scrap-

5. Earl W. Clark, Hoyt S. Haddock, and Stanley J. Volens, *The U.S. Merchant Marine Today: Sunrise or Sunset?* (Washington, D.C.: Labor-Management Maritime Committee, 1970), p. 3.

6. Ibid., pp. 139–45.

7. The National Defense Reserve Fleet is a large collection of government-owned merchant vessels that are kept in lay-up around the country for use in times of sudden need. Many vessels were broken out of reserve to alleviate a worldwide shortage of shipping after the Suez Canal was closed in 1956. More than 170 vessels were activated in the middle of the 1960s to carry supplies to U.S. armed forces in Vietnam. The condition of the fleet has deteriorated lately, and many vessels have been sold for scrap. Between December 31, 1969, and July 1, 1974, the fleet declined from 902 vessels of 8,034,000 deadweight tons to 353 vessels of 3,186,000 deadweight tons. On July 1, 1974, it included 36.6 percent of all U.S. flag oceangoing vessels of 1,000 gross tons and over and 22.9 percent of their total deadweight tonnage. (Data from U.S. Maritime Administration, Office of Subsidy Administration.)

yard. There were some efficient, up-to-date vessels in the fleet—including some of the most modern anywhere—but these were in the minority. It was clear that unless public funds were provided to build new vessels the United States fleet would shrink still further.

The postwar decline, which so disturbed many maritime leaders, could hardly have been avoided, though it might have been moderated with decisive government intervention. U.S. maritime supremacy at the end of the war was a historical anomaly attributable only to Hitler. One must search back to the days of sail and wooden ships to find the last time when the United States possessed a sizable merchant marine capable of competing on even terms with the world's other fleets. U.S. shipyards were no better off. They had not been major suppliers to foreign markets since before the American Civil War. Since the nineteenth century, both industries had prospered only in protected markets or with the aid of subsidies.[8] It is interesting to speculate why this was so, why in these lines of endeavor the American people should have been singularly unsuccessful, whereas in other enterprises they have done very well indeed. Government restrictions on the hiring of personnel and the buying of equipment have no doubt laid a heavy burden on the shipping industry. Whatever the reasons, the Second World War gave the U.S. industries no lasting advantage. After other nations had got back on their feet, the U.S. shipping and shipbuilding industries were once again noncompetitive.

"The root of the problem," wrote Robert D. Calkins in 1966, "is that the operating and construction costs of American ships are higher than those of any other major maritime nation, whereas the productivity of American and foreign flag ships are approximately equal."[9] The situation has improved since the mid-1960s, and for the first time in many years an air of optimism prevails in some sectors of the U.S. maritime community. To some extent the optimism is spurious, so far as it is attribut-

8. Readers wishing to know more about the history of these industries should consult John G. B. Hutchins, *The American Maritime Industries and Public Policy, 1789–1914: An Economic History* (Harvard University Press, 1941; reprinted by Russell & Russell, 1969).

9. In Samuel A. Lawrence, *United States Merchant Shipping Policies and Politics* (Brookings Institution, 1966), foreword, p. vii. Strictly speaking Calkins was wrong: the root of the problem must be sought in the reasons why the U.S. industries are so unproductive—whether because of obsolete work rules, insufficient capital, obstreperous labor, unprogressive management, or similar conditions. The statement that costs are high and productivity is low is not an explanation, merely an observation.

able merely to the large increases in government assistance that followed the passage of a new merchant marine act in 1970 rather than to a fundamental improvement in the competitive position of the industries. That there has been some improvement is undeniable. Maritime unions have helped to lower operating costs by agreeing to reductions in manning aboard new U.S. flag vessels. Labor-management relations are more harmonious than they were several years ago. In some novel services— notably container services—several American steamship operators now compete successfully against foreign lines without the help of operating subsidies. U.S. shipyards still cannot build merchant vessels as cheaply as yards overseas, but the difference in cost, expressed as a fraction of the American cost, fell in the early 1970s. The devaluations of the dollar in 1971 and 1973 have enhanced the competitiveness of both U.S. industries.

Despite these qualifications Calkins's observation is still valid. Costs may have fallen and productivity risen relative to the costs and productivity of foreign competitors; but in 1974 a wide gap remained. Without continuing and substantial government assistance, the U.S. maritime industries would still be unable to compete with foreign producers.

The low productivity of the U.S. maritime industries would not handicap them intolerably if the markets for their products were naturally protected. By naturally protected, I mean that customers were effectively obliged to patronize the local industries, either because the product or production process required it (as American buyers of new buildings must patronize the American construction industry), or because costs of transport, lack of information, or even persistent habits and traditions kept markets local. No constraints of this kind apply to the shipbuilding or shipping industries. In both industries producers actively compete across national boundaries, and customers commonly buy from foreign producers. A large American oil company may one time order a tanker from a Japanese shipyard, another time one from a U.K. shipyard, a third time one from a Danish shipyard, allotting its custom as price, date of delivery, and other considerations dictate, including some considerations that may not be explicitly commercial. Exporters and importers are often indifferent to the nationality of the vessel that carries their goods, if the freight rate is fixed, as it typically is, and if all vessels enjoy the same reputation for punctuality, care of cargo, and the like.

These remarks may be summarized in the language of economists by saying that demand for the products of the U.S. maritime industries would be highly elastic in the absence of legal or other restraints on the freedom of consumers to choose their suppliers, and that if U.S. producers had to offer their product at prices much above those of foreign producers they could scarcely survive in free competition.

Previous Studies

It is impossible to write of U.S. maritime aids without acknowledging a large debt to Samuel A. Lawrence and his *United States Merchant Shipping Policies and Politics*. Lawrence's book is not an economic study of the assistance program; but his account of relations between the government and the shipping industry during the postwar period has been invaluable.

Economists have paid surprisingly little attention, especially in recent years, to the many federal aids given the U.S. maritime industries. Although it is nearly two decades old, Wytze Gorter's study of U.S. shipping policy contains much interesting material about the assistance program.[10] The most extensive work was written by a group of Northwestern University economists around 1960.[11] This study, which is still highly useful, evaluated many of the effects of the assistance program and attempted to decide whether the economic value of the merchant fleet was large enough to justify so substantial a program of government aid. My book differs from theirs chiefly in looking at a broader range of aids and in paying less attention to such specific effects as those on ship design, labor costs, and freight rates.

A number of reports on maritime assistance have been prepared during the past fifteen years by official bodies. Although these rarely contain any critical analysis, they occasionally include useful information not easily found elsewhere. The congressional committees that oversee the program have not recently shown much disposition to scrutinize it, but the records of their hearings are a rich mine of valuable information.[12]

10. Wytze Gorter, *United States Shipping Policy* (Harper for the Council on Foreign Relations, 1956).
11. Allen R. Ferguson and others, *The Economic Value of the United States Merchant Marine* (Northwestern University, Transportation Center, 1961).
12. For example, an excellent discussion of U.S. requirements for merchant shipping, the domestic industry's need for public assistance, and the many forms in which assistance is given may be found in the statement of Nicholas Johnson, then maritime administrator, in *Vietnam—Shipping Policy Review,* Hearings before the Subcommittee on Merchant Marine of the House Committee on Merchant Marine and Fisheries, 89 Cong. 2 sess. (1966), pt. 2, pp. 346–64.

Plan of the Book

The plan of this book is as follows. Chapter 2 briefly reviews the various forms of public assistance that governments here and abroad give their maritime industries. Examples of many of them are to be found in the U.S. maritime program.

The most important maritime aids are discussed in chapters 3 through 7. Chapter 3 covers the operating differential subsidy, one of the most open and familiar forms of U.S. maritime assistance. The construction differential subsidy is discussed in chapter 4. The cabotage laws and the advantage they afford to the U.S. maritime industries are the subject of chapter 5. Chapter 6 is devoted to subsidies that are given to the maritime industries through the federal tax system. The U.S. cargo preference laws are treated in chapter 7.

Chapters 8 and 9 critically examine some of the commonly advanced reasons for government assistance to the maritime industries. The economic justifications for maritime assistance, including its employment, output, and balance of payments effects, are discussed in chapter 8. The argument that the nation's security requires a maritime program of the kind we have now is examined in chapter 9.

The book ends with a summary and conclusions in chapter 10.

CHAPTER TWO

Forms of Maritime Assistance

IN ORDER TO ACHIEVE certain economic objectives and to safeguard the nation's security, the federal government has determined that the United States must have a domestic flag merchant marine capable of carrying a sizable fraction of the nation's oceanborne commerce, and a domestic shipbuilding industry to furnish vessels to the merchant marine. The nature of the maritime industries explains why government intervention in private markets is necessary to achieve these objectives. Once the government has decided to intervene, the question then follows: What form should this intervention take?

Diversity of Aids Available

Governments have at their command a broad selection of instruments for providing assistance to local maritime industries.[1] Such aids can be classified as either fiscal or nonfiscal in character. The U.S. maritime assistance program provides examples of both.

Fiscal aids are defined here to cover all forms of assistance that are rendered through the exercise of a government's taxing or spending powers. Usually they involve money flows between the government and the private sector, though payments in kind are also included. Money payments may be for goods or services, or for no consideration whatever: "unrequited payments," as Shoup terms them.[2]

1. Descriptions of maritime subsidies around the world are collected in U.S. Maritime Administration, *Maritime Subsidies* (U.S. Government Printing Office, 1974). This section draws heavily upon that report.

For an admirable review of this subject, with copious references to historical practice, see John G. B. Hutchins, *The American Maritime Industries and Public Policy, 1789–1914: An Economic History* (Harvard University Press, 1941; reprinted by Russell & Russell, 1969), chap. 2.

2. Carl S. Shoup, *Public Finance* (Aldine, 1969), p. 145. Shoup uses the term only in connection with payments from the government to the private sector; it is used here more generally to include flows in the opposite direction also, in the form of tax payments.

Nonfiscal assistance is rendered through the exercise of a government's regulatory powers. No payments flow between the government and the private sector, either of money or in kind. All forms of nonfiscal assistance are fundamentally alike. In every case the government carves out a protected market for the domestic industry. How this is done is what distinguishes one form of assistance from another.

Nonfiscal Aids

The earliest government aids to the maritime industries were probably nonfiscal aids in the form of cabotage laws that reserved a nation's coastal trade to ships of the national fleet. Such laws are still common throughout the world. Shipbuilding industries were aided by restricting national registry to locally built vessels. Both forms of assistance have been practiced in this country from the earliest days of the federal government.[3]

Although the right of every state to reserve its coastal trade to nationals is well established in international law, no corresponding right to reserve a nation's foreign trade is recognized. The reason is obvious: it would be impossible for all nations to accomplish this object together, and the attempt of any single country to do so would bring it into conflict with its trading partners. Nonetheless, many nations do attempt to reserve a part of their foreign trade to national vessels, though seldom, if ever, all of it. The United States is one, using as its instrument the cargo preference laws.

Cargo preference laws are an excellent example of nonfiscal assistance. They differ from country to country chiefly in the variety of cargoes they cover and in the fraction of those cargoes that they require to move in ships of the national fleet. It may be taken for granted that all cargo preference laws cover goods and services that governments buy for their own account. If they went no further they would be a form of fiscal assistance, because payments are made from the government to the carriers. But the preference laws of most nations, including the United States, also extend to commercial shipments in which the government is in some way involved. The role of government in a modern economy is so pervasive that with a little imagination laws might be written that would affect a

3. Federal law still reserves the coasting trade to U.S. flag and U.S.–built ships, but foreign-built ships have been admitted to U.S. registry since 1912 for service in the foreign trades. See chapter 5 for a discussion of the U.S. cabotage laws.

great many shipping transactions, by finding in them some element, however slight or insubstantial, of government participation. The United States
has resisted the temptation to do this better than some other nations. The
U.S. preference laws affect only a small fraction of the nation's commerce;
the government's interest has to be substantial or meaningful before the
cargoes are subject to the preference requirements; and, except for military cargoes, only half of certain classes of cargo that are subject to the
laws (called "government-impelled cargo") have to move in U.S. flag
bottoms.[4]

Elsewhere in the world, especially in South America, the scope of
these laws is frequently broader. They often embrace a wider class of
goods than the preference laws of the United States. In at least one country the preference laws apparently extend to cargoes arising in purely
commercial transactions, without even a pretense of government involvement. Often they require *all* affected cargoes to travel in ships of the
national fleet, although reciprocity agreements with other nations may
provide for a division of cargoes between ships of the importing and exporting countries.

Another form of nonfiscal assistance to shipping industries, closely
related to cargo preference, is the bilateral agreement that reserves the
commerce between two nations to ships of their national fleets, generally
in equal shares. Unlike the cargo preference laws, bilateral agreements
usually control the transport of all cargoes moving between two countries,
not just government-impelled cargoes. A particular agreement may benefit
the merchant marine of only one country, if the merchant marine of the
other had previously carried most of the trade between them. Or it may
benefit the fleets of both countries, if most of the trade had moved aboard
ships of third countries.

Bilateral agreements are an increasingly popular form of nonfiscal
assistance, to the dismay of some major maritime nations whose ships
depend on much third-country carriage.[5] The agreements are especially

4. Between 1963 and 1971, however, the federal government insisted that one-
half of all wheat and certain other grains sold for export to the Soviet Union and
most other Eastern European countries should be delivered abroad in U.S. flag
vessels, regardless of whether the government was involved in their sale. Lately
efforts have been made, so far unsuccessfully, to bring other cargoes—chiefly imports
of oil and petroleum products—within the compass of these laws.

For a discussion of the U.S. cargo preference laws, see chapter 7.

5. Third-country carriage is the transport of cargo between two nations, neither
of which is the carrier's country of registry.

popular with several South American countries that use them to increase the tonnage their merchant marines carry. The United States concluded its first bilateral agreement—and so far its only one—in October 1972 with the Soviet Union. It provided that henceforth one-third of the commerce between the two nations would be carried in U.S. flag vessels and one-third in Soviet vessels, with one-third left for third-country carriers.

Fiscal Aids

Fiscal aids are much more varied in character than nonfiscal aids. Their one common feature is that all are administered through an exercise of the government's taxing or spending powers and therefore usually involve money flows between the public and private sectors. Occasionally the payments are made for a consideration, as when the government buys ships from builders or shipping services from operators. But for the most part these aids take the form of unrequited payments: taxes if paid from the private to the public sector, subsidies if paid in the opposite direction.

It is convenient to distinguish fiscal from nonfiscal aids in this manner, but in practice the distinction often is blurred. The cargo preference laws discussed above, for instance, have both fiscal and nonfiscal characteristics. If they only require that public authorities should patronize domestic flag vessels and refrain from using foreign flag carriers, they are fiscal aids, because the benefits are given through an exercise of the government's spending powers. If they only require that certain classes of private shippers should patronize domestic carriers, they constitute a form of nonfiscal assistance. Most preference laws, however, have both requirements.

Another example of this mix of fiscal and nonfiscal assistance comes from early U.S. history. Before foreign vessels were barred from the U.S. coasting trade in 1817, they were already effectively excluded by the imposition of severely discriminatory tonnage duties on foreign flag vessels. A tax is definitely a fiscal instrument, but when it is imposed at prohibitive rates its effect is the same as that of a prohibition by fiat, and the difference between fiscal and nonfiscal assistance vanishes. In this case the tax generates no revenue; hence, the presence or absence of a flow of money from the private to the public sector cannot be a criterion of fiscal assistance.[6]

6. Some persons might accordingly conclude that fiscal aids should be redefined to include only assistance that is accompanied by a flow of money between the two

In practice there is little risk of confusing these aids. Apparently no major nation today protects its merchant marine or shipbuilding industry by imposing prohibitive taxes on foreign competitors. But various taxes are used, at lower rates, to favor local industry. A government may protect its shipbuilders by imposing a duty on foreign-built vessels when owners present them for registry. The attractiveness of such a duty is diminished, however, by the ease with which shipowners can register vessels under other flags. No shipowner would consider registering his vessel in a country with high duties unless he had a reason for wanting that flag of registry—if he wished, for example, to carry cargoes controlled by that country. A nation that persisted in taxing foreign-built vessels might not only fail to protect its own shipbuilding industry but also gradually lose its merchant marine.

The United States imposes no duty on merchant vessels of foreign construction that are registered in this country for service in the foreign trades. (Their use in the domestic trades is forbidden by the cabotage laws.) It does impose a high rate of duty on the repairs made on U.S. flag vessels in foreign countries, and on equipment and materials procured abroad for such repairs. They are dutiable at an ad valorem rate of 50 percent, unless the owner can show that the work was necessary to secure the immediate safety of the vessel.[7]

Taxes on shipping services that are designed to assist the domestic flag marine can assume several forms. Perhaps the simplest is a special surcharge upon imported goods carried in foreign flag vessels. Congress enacted a discriminatory duty many years ago, but authorized the President to refrain from imposing it upon goods arriving aboard foreign flag vessels registered in countries that do not discriminate against U.S. flag vessels.[8] In practice the U.S. duty is apparently a dead letter.

But other forms of discrimination are possible. Higher tonnage duties can be imposed on foreign flag vessels; or higher charges can be levied for the use of a country's navigational facilities. Discriminatory port or consular fees can be charged against foreign flag vessels. It is just possible

---

sectors. All other aids would be considered nonfiscal in form. The idea has merit, but would create other distinctions hardly less arbitrary than those the above classification of assistance is meant to avoid: the distinction, for example, between one tax that yields no revenue at all and another that yields very little.

7. 19 U.S.C. 1970 edition, sec. 1466.

8. 19 U.S.C. 1970 edition, sec. 128; 46 U.S.C. 1970 edition, secs. 141, 146.

that a country might levy a tax on its citizens' purchases of foreign shipping services (though I know of no instance in which this has been done). It would be a difficult tax to administer, since the value of transport is often concealed in the prices of goods, such as those bought on a c.i.f. basis.[9] Furthermore, authorities might fear that such a tax would discourage the nation's exports.

Subsidies to a country's maritime industries are probably a more common and certainly a more significant form of fiscal assistance throughout the world than discriminatory taxes on foreign competitors. Subsidies are unquestionably more important in the United States, where the only instance of a discriminatory tax is the 50 percent duty on ship repairs performed abroad. Shipbuilding subsidies are especially common. Few countries, it seems, calculate the size of their shipbuilding subsidies as methodically as the United States.[10] Some governments simply assume a part of the construction costs when vessels are built in local shipyards. Other governments extend cheap lines of credit to purchasers. It is a nice question whether some of these subsidies might not equally be called subsidies to shipowners, since their effect is to lower the price of new merchant vessels. In fact, many governments give subsidies even for locally built ships that are to be registered abroad. If the subsidy is not limited to ships for the domestic flag marine, it is hard to call it a subsidy to local shipowners, since its advantages are equally available to their competitors abroad.[11] In practice, of course, nationals may buy more local ships than their foreign counterparts, and therefore benefit most from local construction subsidies.

Subsidies to ship operators are also widespread and extremely diverse. The government may underwrite the annual deficit of a publicly owned steamship line. Or it may subsidize private investment in new merchant vessels, either by making outright grants in amounts equal to some fraction of the vessel's cost, by administering a subsidy through the nation's tax system, or by a variety of indirect subsidies, such as loan guarantees, cheap lines of credit, generous trade-in allowances, and the like.

9. C.i.f. (cost, insurance, and freight) denotes a price that includes the cost of the merchandise, the freight charges to a specific destination, and the insurance on the shipment of goods. F.o.b. (free on board), on the other hand, denotes a price that includes all costs up to a certain point of departure or stage of delivery including packing, transportation, and insurance.
10. See chapter 4 for a discussion of the U.S. construction differential subsidy.
11. On the other hand, one might describe it as a subsidy to the world shipping industry.

Every imaginable type of subsidy, except for the most bizarre and implausible, has probably been tried somewhere, sometime. Tax subsidies alone vary considerably. Some take the form of special depreciation allowances that shipowners may deduct from taxable income the first year after investment, an advantage that is offset in certain cases by smaller deductions later. Some tax subsidies, as in the United States, may involve intricate mechanisms for borrowing tax moneys from public authorities to invest in new ships, with deferred, interest-free repayment provisions.[12]

Subsidies to shipowners for the purchase of new vessels may in some cases just as well be called subsidies to shipbuilders, exactly as some shipbuilding subsidies are in principle hardly distinguishable from subsidies to shipowners, and for the same reasons. Only if the shipowner can use his construction subsidy, however given, toward the purchase of foreign-built vessels is one justified in calling it unequivocally an aid to domestic shipowners instead of to domestic shipbuilders.

The regular payments governments make to shipping lines to cover a part of the lines' operating expenses appear to be somewhat less common than capital subsidies and are certainly less common in the most important maritime nations. Possibly the most forthright and systematic program of such operating subsidies anywhere is the one administered in the United States, which has lasted nearly four decades and has maintained a sizable fleet of oceangoing vessels at a public cost of nearly $4 billion. The operating subsidy is one of the most important aids the federal government gives the U.S. shipping industry and is thoroughly discussed in chapter 3.

Operating subsidies are also used by other nations. Some simply meet the deficits of their national shipping lines. Others pay fixed sums annually to shipping operators. Still others subsidize their carriers in less direct ways—by awarding mail contracts, for example, that call for larger payments than the cost of the service warrants, or by paying a part of carriers' contributions to social security funds for seafarers. It is not uncommon for countries to subsidize transportation between the mainland and remote islands whose population is too poor or too small to support the service alone. But whether such payments should be regarded as subsidies to the domestic flag marine is questionable, since they are so obviously intended to benefit the islanders rather than the carriers.

12. See chapter 6 for a discussion of the maritime tax subsidies in the United States.

CHAPTER THREE

The Operating Differential Subsidy

OF THE MANY PUBLIC AIDS to the U.S. maritime industries, the operating differential subsidy is the most visible form of assistance and one of the most important. It was established, along with several others, by the Merchant Marine Act of 1936.[1]

The sources of the 1936 act can be traced back to the 1920s and 1930s, when the government tried to foster a privately owned merchant marine that could take over the shipping lines it had organized after the First World War. The aim was to create a commercially viable merchant marine that would also serve the needs of the country. Despite some progress toward this goal, it soon became evident that no privately owned U.S. merchant marine could compete on equal terms with foreign competitors. Congress responded with the Merchant Marine Act of 1928, which provided public subsidies to private shipping lines through the award of lucrative mail contracts. But the program was a failure. Contracts were awarded without regard to the needs of U.S. shippers or the postal service. Extravagant awards were made to established operators. There was scandal when some members of the U.S. Shipping Board, which was responsible for selling the government lines, were identified too closely with prospective buyers attracted by the subsidy. Improvements in administration came belatedly and failed to satisfy congressional critics, many of whom were hostile to any subsidy system.[2]

1. 49 Stat. 1985. The 1936 act and subsequent amendments are presented in *The Merchant Marine Act, 1936, the Shipping Act, 1916, and Related Acts (As Amended through the 91st Congress 2nd Session)*, for the House Committee on Merchant Marine and Fisheries, 91 Cong. 2 sess. (1970). For a history of the statute, see Samuel A. Lawrence, *United States Merchant Shipping Policies and Politics* (Brookings Institution, 1966), chap. 2, or Paul M. Zeis, *American Shipping Policy* (Princeton University Press, 1938), chap. 12.

2. The history of the 1928 program is recounted in Zeis, *American Shipping Policy*, chap. 10.

This unsavory experience led to studies and investigations both within Congress and without that culminated in the Merchant Marine Act of 1936. The act itself was a compromise that took months to evolve. Many issues had to be settled; but the basic issue was whether the government should support a privately owned fleet or acquire and operate its own. At length Congress opted for private ownership, supported by a program of public subsidies, openly provided and protected by safeguards against waste and misappropriation.

The subsidy system has proved remarkably durable. Few important changes were made in the operating program for more than three decades —until passage of the Merchant Marine Act of 1970. Even in 1974 its most significant features are much the same as they were in the thirties. The authors of the 1936 act determined that operating subsidies should be provided to a limited number of American shipping companies; that the companies should provide regular service over certain vital shipping routes in U.S. foreign commerce; that the subsidies should be carefully calculated to just offset the lower costs of the operators' foreign competitors; and that the companies receiving subsidies should be closely supervised to guard against abuses.[3] Of these principles only the one that limited subsidies to liners operating on established trade routes has been substantially modified.

The 1936 act also established a United States Maritime Commission to administer the new shipping program and assigned to it a variety of functions.[4] The commission lasted until 1950, when it was abolished by executive order and its responsibilities were divided among other agencies. Its promotional duties went to a new Maritime Administration in the Department of Commerce, headed by a maritime administrator (since 1970 the assistant secretary of commerce for maritime affairs), while its

3. Several of these ideas were anticipated in earlier acts. For example, the Merchant Marine Act of 1920 directed the U.S. Shipping Board to determine what steamship lines should be established between this country and world markets that the board thought were "desirable for the promotion, development, expansion, and maintenance of the foreign . . . trade of the United States" (41 Stat. 991, sec. 7). Practically the same language was used in the 1936 act, "essential," however, being substituted for "desirable," and the reference being to routes rather than markets.

The policy of tailoring the size of the subsidy to the difference in costs between U.S. and foreign operators was followed in the award of ocean-mail contracts under the ill-fated Merchant Marine Act of 1928, after early revelations of waste and mismanagement. See Lawrence, *U.S. Merchant Shipping*, p. 44.

4. See Lawrence, *U.S. Merchant Shipping*, pp. 67–75, for a description of these functions and the commission's early work.

regulatory duties were assumed by the Federal Maritime Board (superseded in 1961, with some reshuffling of functions, by the Federal Maritime Commission). It is the Maritime Administration that currently administers the maritime subsidies, and it is this body whose work is of chief interest here.

For many years only liner services—passenger as well as cargo—on what the act terms "essential" trade routes in U.S. foreign commerce were eligible for subsidy. Liners serve as common carriers, sailing along fixed routes on regular schedules and accepting cargoes from many different shippers for delivery at ports along their routes. Irregular carriers differ from liners in their readiness to sail wherever business takes them. The law was changed in 1970 to permit subsidy payments for certain other services described below, but the bulk of all subsidies are still paid for liner operations.

The law directs the Maritime Administration to determine which trade routes are essential in U.S. foreign commerce and to contract with U.S. citizens for service on these routes. The Maritime Administration agrees to pay the carriers an operating differential subsidy, and the carriers bind themselves to provide not less than a specified number of sailings per year. They must use American-built vessels that are registered under the U.S. flag and crewed by U.S. citizens.

The Maritime Administration enjoys wide latitude in determining what services are essential in U.S. foreign commerce. The language of the 1936 act provides little guidance in making this determination, although it enjoins the administration, in so many words, not to be extravagant. In practice, every route on which a substantial volume of foreign commerce moves to or from this country has been identified as an "essential" route.

In 1974 there are twenty-seven trade routes, five trade areas, two round-the-world services, and a tricontinent service that are deemed by the Maritime Administration to be essential for U.S. foreign commerce within the meaning of the 1936 act.[5] Of these thirty-five "routes" (as they may be called for convenience) twenty-seven are served by U.S. flag lines on regular schedules, many by more than one line. Subsidies are provided to eleven operators for service on twenty-four routes. It seems that in planning its administration of the subsidy program soon after the 1936 act was passed, the Maritime Commission envisioned that only one

5. Data supplied by U.S. Maritime Administration, Office of Subsidy Administration.

operator on any route would be subsidized.[6] In 1974, twelve trade routes are served by two or more operators receiving subsidy payments, and of these twelve, five routes are served by three or more.

Description of the Subsidy

The word "differential" exactly expresses the principle of the operating differential subsidy. The payments that are made to U.S. operators are intended to offset the difference between the high costs they must pay to operate U.S. flag vessels and the lower costs of their foreign competitors. This is sometimes referred to as the "parity principle": the subsidy should equate costs of foreign and domestic operators. Even with the best will in the world, however, it is only possible to approximate this ideal, owing to the extreme difficulty of discovering the costs of foreign operators.

Operating Expenses Covered

Until 1970, the Merchant Marine Act of 1936 explicitly recognized five items of operating expense that were likely to cost the operators of U.S. flag vessels more than they cost their foreign competitors: insurance, maintenance, repairs not compensated for by insurance, wages, and subsistence of officers and crew. Subsistence was deleted from subsidizable expenses, except in the case of passenger vessels, in 1970. The act provides that each contractor shall be paid an amount not greater than the excess of the "fair and reasonable cost" of these items over the estimated cost of the same items if the contractor's vessels were operated under the flag of a "substantial" foreign competitor. No guidance is provided for determining what costs are fair and reasonable, how a competitor's costs are to be estimated, or what is substantial competition. In addition, the act authorizes the Maritime Administration to pay a differential subsidy on any other items of expense whose higher cost puts the contractor at a substantial disadvantage with its foreign competitors and to grant an additional subsidy whenever necessary to offset government aid to foreign competitors; but no payments have ever been made under either provision.

Operating differential subsidies are computed separately for each trade route. In every case the Maritime Administration determines as best it

6. Lawrence, *U.S. Merchant Shipping,* p. 71.

can the operating costs of the contractor's principal foreign competitors, limiting its attention to those items of expense that may be subsidized. An effort is made to compare like with like, by making this determination only for a vessel that is approximately comparable to the contractor's own vessels. If none are comparable, the expenses are calculated for a hypothetical vessel that is. For each item of expense the same procedure is followed. The difference is calculated between each competitor's cost and the contractor's cost; a weighted average is computed of the differences, with weights that reflect the importance of the competitors; and the difference is expressed as a fraction of the contractor's own expense. This then determines the subsidy rate.[7]

Once the subsidy rate is determined, the amount of subsidy that is due the operator is calculated as the product of the rate and the operator's expenses. The calculation is repeated for each subsidizable item.

Size of Subsidizable Expenses

Much the largest subsidizable expense—and the one that accounts for the lion's share of subsidy expenditures on all trade routes—is the wages of officers and crew. Table 3-1 records the voyage expenses of all cargo ships in subsidized service during 1969. Wages amounted to 30.2 percent of total voyage expenses. Insurance, maintenance and repairs (which are always lumped together in subsidy calculations), and subsistence were much less costly, adding up to just 13.6 percent of total expenses. These are average figures; the proportions vary by type of ship and trade route sailed.

The total amounts expended in subsidy depend not only on the size of each item in an operator's account but on the subsidy rate as well. The average rate of subsidy for cargo ships on all trade routes in 1969, by item of expense, was: wages, 67.3 percent; insurance, 28.7 percent; maintenance and repairs, 27.6 percent; and subsistence, 18.1 percent.[8] Again wages rank first. Of every dollar of wages paid aboard cargo ships in subsidized service during 1969, about 67 cents was paid by the federal government. The combination of a high subsidy rate and large expendi-

---

7. A more detailed description of this procedure, with examples, is given in Allen R. Ferguson and others, *The Economic Value of the United States Merchant Marine* (Northwestern University, Transportation Center, 1961), pp. 45–49.

8. These figures were provisional and may have been adjusted slightly before the last subsidy payments were made for voyages completed in 1969.

Table 3-1. Voyage Expenses, Subsidy Rates, and Subsidy Accruals,
U.S. Flag Cargo Ships in Subsidized Service, 1969[a]

Amounts in thousands of dollars

	Voyage expenses		Subsidy rate (percent)	Subsidy accruals	
Expense item	Amount	Percentage of total		Amount	Percentage of total
Vessel operating					
expenses	**344,414**	**51.5**	...	...	...
Wages, total	201,833	30.2	67.3	135,843	84.6
Straight time	80,063	12.0	...	...	...
Overtime	42,013	6.3	...	...	...
Other[b]	79,757	11.9	...	...	...
Insurance, total	45,317	6.8	...	...	...
Hull and					
machinery	16,686	2.5	28.7	12,825	8.0
Protection and					
indemnity	27,968	4.2	...	...	...
Other	662	0.1	...	...	...
Maintenance and					
repairs	36,787	5.5	27.6	10,147	6.3
Fuel	34,999	5.2	...	...	...
Stores, supplies,					
equipment	12,003	1.8	...	...	...
Subsistence	9,576	1.4	18.1	1,734	1.1
Other operating	3,899	0.6	...	...	...
Port[c]	**61,862**	**9.3**	...	...	...
Cargo[d]	**231,115**	**34.6**	...	...	...
Brokerage	**6,631**	**1.0**	...	...	...
Other voyage	**24,227**	**3.6**	...	...	...
Voyage, total	**668,249**	**100.0**	...	**160,550**	**100.0**

Sources: U.S. Maritime Administration, Office of Subsidy Administration, unpublished tables.
a. In addition to the cargo ship subsidies shown here, accrued subsidies for the operation of four combination cargo-passenger ships and nine passenger ships amounted to $45,928,000 in 1969.
b. Payroll taxes, pension and welfare fund payments, and the like.
c. Pilotage, wharfage, mooring fees, and the like.
d. Stevedoring, lighterage, and the like.

tures by contractors means that the bulk of subsidy accruals is in respect of wages—84.6 percent in 1969 (column 5). The dollar amounts of the accruals (shown in column 4) are tentative, being subject to final determination of the subsidy rates and to final audit of the contractors' accounts. If payments are made in the amount of the accruals, they will cover 24.0 percent of voyage expenses, and account for 19.6 percent of operators' revenues.

Changes Made in 1970

The Merchant Marine Act of 1970 made a number of changes, both large and small, in the operating subsidy program. In addition to ending subsidies for subsistence, Congress considered the recommendation of the Maritime Administration that subsidies for maintenance and repairs should also be eliminated. But the objections of labor and management groups in shipbuilding prevailed, and Congress declined to act.

A more important change affected the way in which wage subsidies are calculated. Before 1970, the amount of subsidy to be paid to an operator had been determined in accordance with the parity principle. As applied to wage costs, this meant that the government must pay the operator of a U.S. flag vessel the difference between the higher wages of his American officers and crew (provided that the wages were "fair and reasonable") and the lower wages paid by his foreign competitor. It also meant that when new wage agreements were negotiated, any increase in wages was borne by the federal government.

This arrangement was unsatisfactory for several reasons. It was plain to everyone that operators had little incentive to be tough bargainers in wage negotiations with maritime unions. Operators would bear the cost of any strike, but the additional cost of a more generous settlement that might avert a strike—or end one—would be borne in full by the federal government. This lack of symmetry became more and more noxious as wage costs, and wage subsidies, soared in the 1960s.

In theory, the government's interests might have been protected by measuring all wage claims against the fair and reasonable standard and disallowing those that incorporated exorbitant wage increases. In practice, it would be folly to suppose that the Maritime Administration could have dictated its notions of fairness and reasonableness to the shipping industry. For years it did not even try. Early in the postwar period, when the wages of shipboard labor were thought to have fallen below those paid in comparable shoreside employment, the Maritime Administration acquiesced in the wage increases negotiated between the operators and unions and refrained from finding any wage payments to be in excess of what was fair and reasonable. In 1955, however, Congress admonished the Maritime Administration to pay more heed to the standard and scrutinize operators' wage claims more critically. Ten years later the Maritime Subsidy Board, which must pass on such matters, disallowed a part of the wage claims filed by the operators on the grounds that the wage increases they had agreed to were excessive and that the wages they were paying contravened the standard.

The secretary of commerce overruled the board's decision, but served notice that, in future, wages established in collective bargaining agreements would be tested by the fair and reasonable standard more rigorously than before. At this point, the Maritime Administration began looking for another criterion—a search that led to development of the wage index system.

In 1971 the Maritime Administration began paying operators the difference between an amount called their "subsidizable wage costs" and the estimated wage costs of their foreign competitors. An operator's subsidizable wage costs are initially equal to true wage costs, less any expenses disallowed by the Maritime Administration. Each year thereafter his subsidizable wage costs are adjusted in phase with changes in a newly created index of wage rates for workers in other industries. If seamen's wages increase faster than the wage index, he pays the difference himself; if they increase less rapidly, he keeps the difference. To limit both profits and losses, the plan provides that subsidizable wage costs may not fall short of 90 percent or exceed 110 percent of an operator's true wage costs. Every few years the subsidizable wage costs are to be readjusted if they stray too far from the operator's actual costs and brought back to within a specified few percentage points of the true costs.

Extending the Program to Bulk Carriers

The most important change made by the 1970 act was the opening of the operating subsidy program to U.S. vessels in bulk cargo carrying services. Bulk carriers offer a very different service from that of cargo liners. They are not common carriers; the terms of their service are fixed by contract between operator and shipper. Typically they are chartered for one or more voyages to carry a single cargo occupying much of their capacity, such as a shipload of ore, oil, or grain. Nowadays some new bulk vessels, including tankers, are chartered for periods of years by a single shipper, such as an oil company, even before the vessel's keel is laid. Indeed, without the assurance of such a charter many shipowners would refuse to risk their capital in a large new ship.

Because of these differences it was necessary to strike many of the references to trade routes from the 1936 act and replace them with the words "essential services," to bring bulk cargo carrying services within the compass of the act.

The portion of the statute that authorizes subsidy payments to bulk carriers fails to spell out how the subsidies should be calculated. This omission reflects the atmosphere of good feeling in which the maritime legislation of 1970 was passed. In 1936 Congress determined that there should be no repetition of the scandals that had marred the subsidy program a few years before, and so it carefully specified in the 1936 act how large the subsidies should be. The situation was different in 1970. Congressional opinion favored a large expansion of aid to the maritime industries. The operating subsidy program had been well administered throughout the postwar period, without any hint of misconduct. No groups counseled prudence and caution in opposition to the maritime interests that were agitating for an extension of subsidies to bulk carriers. Accordingly there was no pressure upon legislative draftsmen to write stringent safeguards into the act.

As for the Maritime Administration, it had no experience subsidizing irregular operations and admitted to Congress in 1970 that it could suggest no statutory language for regulating subsidies to bulk operators that would be as particular as the language already in the act relating to cargo liners. It therefore favored language affording it maximum freedom to devise an appropriate subsidy program. Congress obliged, and the law gives the Maritime Administration discretion to pay whatever subsidy is needed "to make the cost of operating [a vessel in an essential bulk cargo carrying service] competitive with the cost of operating similar vessels under the registry of a foreign country."[9]

By mid-1974 it is still unclear what practices the Maritime Administration is to follow. With the exception of the subsidies given to U.S. bulk carriers to deliver American grain to the Soviet Union in 1972 and 1973, no major subsidy program has yet been developed for bulk cargo carriers. The contracts that have been concluded for subsidized service beginning in 1974 apparently leave it till later to decide how the subsidies are to be computed.

Growth of Bulk Shipments

To understand why the operating subsidy program was opened to bulk carriers, it is necessary to understand how the composition of U.S. exports

9. Merchant Marine Act of 1970, sec. 16(5), 84 Stat. 1023.

**Table 3-2. Volume of U.S. Oceanborne Foreign Trade,
by Class of Carrier, 1956–72**

Millions of long tons

Calendar year	All carriers		Liners		Nonliners		Tankers	
	Total	U.S. flag	Total	U.S. flag	Total	U.S. flag	Total	U.S. flag
1956	260.1	53.9	46.4	18.0	116.0	15.8	97.7	20.1
1957	289.3	50.8	46.7	17.8	135.1	16.2	107.5	16.8
1958	253.3	30.9	43.4	14.0	105.1	8.8	104.8	8.0
1959	267.0	27.1	48.1	13.5	106.9	8.2	112.0	5.4
1960	277.9	31.0	50.7	14.5	109.0	8.4	118.2	8.1
1961	272.4	26.3	49.0	12.6	106.7	7.8	116.7	5.9
1962	296.8	29.6	48.3	12.7	125.2	8.3	123.3	8.5
1963	311.6	28.5	48.9	13.5	136.2	8.2	126.5	6.8
1964	332.8	30.5	50.3	14.2	161.4	9.8	121.1	6.6
1965	371.3	27.7	49.2	11.2	171.6	8.2	150.5	8.2
1966	392.3	26.2	49.9	11.4	189.5	6.9	152.8	7.9
1967	387.6	20.5	47.9	10.6	190.4	5.4	149.3	4.5
1968	418.6	25.0	46.1	11.1	209.5	6.4	163.1	7.5
1969	426.1	19.1	41.0	9.2	211.6	4.4	173.5	5.5
1970	473.2	25.2	50.4	11.8	240.7	5.4	182.1	8.0
1971	457.4	24.4	44.2	10.1	220.7	4.8	192.5	9.5
1972p	446.7	24.6	45.1	10.0	201.4	3.1	200.1	11.5

Sources: *Annual Report of the Maritime Administration for Fiscal Year 1971*, p. 75; *Annual Report of the Maritime Administration for Fiscal Year 1973*, p. 89.
  p. Preliminary data.

and imports has changed during the postwar period. Between 1950 and 1972 the annual volume of U.S. oceanborne foreign commerce nearly quadrupled: from 117.5 million long tons in 1950 to 446.7 million long tons in 1972. But the increase in traffic was not distributed evenly among all classes of carriers. Table 3-2 shows that between 1956 and 1972 the tonnage carried by liners actually decreased by 3 percent; the carriage of dry bulk cargoes increased by 74 percent; while shipments moved by tankers increased by 105 percent.[10] The exact figures are of no particular significance, since shipping volume fluctuates greatly from year to year. What matters most is that shipments of bulk commodities—almost en-

10. The statistics used here to illustrate postwar trends are taken from the 1956–72 period because cargo statistics before 1956 are not broken down finely enough. It is reasonable to assume, however, that the same trends were present in earlier years also.

tirely ore, oil, and grain—have risen dramatically compared with shipments of liner commodities. As a result U.S. flag vessels currently carry a much smaller fraction of the nation's oceanborne commerce than they did two decades ago; for the share of U.S. commerce that moves in U.S. flag vessels is highest in the liner trades, in which many U.S. operators are subsidized, and much lower in the bulk trades, in which until recently no operating subsidies were paid.[11]

The Merchant Marine Act of 1970 reflected the concern that many persons felt over the declining share of U.S. commerce moving in U.S. vessels. Just what share American ships should carry no one can say, but maritime spokesmen have urged that it should be at least 30 percent— preferably 50 percent—of the nation's commerce. The maritime program that President Nixon sent to Congress in 1969 and that resulted in the 1970 act set a goal of 30 percent. This meant including bulk cargo vessels in the subsidy program; for even if U.S. vessels carried *all* cargoes moving in the liner trades, the U.S. share of cargo movements in all trades in 1970 would have increased only from 5.6 percent to 14.6 percent, well short of the established target. In fact, of course, it is unreasonable to suppose that U.S. liners could greatly increase their share of total liner traffic. In order to do so they would have to displace foreign carriers, since exports and imports aboard liners are growing only slowly. On the other hand, U.S. carriers could gradually increase their share of bulk movements without displacing foreign flag carriers simply by claiming a sizable portion of each year's increase in the movement of bulk cargoes.

To illustrate how this might be done, suppose that bulk shipments to and from the United States grow by 6 percent a year betwen 1972 and 1982, while movements by liner remain constant.[12] Suppose further that U.S. vessels are able to capture 80 percent of each year's increase in bulk shipments, meanwhile continuing to carry the 22.2 percent of liner cargoes that moved in U.S. bottoms in 1972. The U.S. share of bulk movements would then increase from 3.6 percent in 1972 to 37.4 percent in 1982, and the U.S. share of all movements, including those aboard liners, would

11. Bulk cargo operators benefit, however, from the U.S. cargo preference laws; see chapter 7.

12. Between 1956 and 1972 tanker shipments actually increased by 4.5 percent a year, and dry bulk shipments by 5.5 percent. Both figures were obtained by fitting a least-squares regression line to the logarithm of annual shipments during the seventeen-year period. Tanker shipments will probably increase faster in the future than they did in the past.

Table 3-3. Share of U.S. Flag Cargo Vessels in U.S. Oceanborne Foreign Trade, by Weight and Value, Selected Years, 1947–71

Percent

Measure	1947	1951	1956	1961	1966	1971
By value	n.a.	n.a.	33.8	25.6	22.5	19.6
By weight	57.6	39.8	20.7	9.7	6.7	5.3

Sources: *Annual Report of the Maritime Administration for Fiscal Year 1971*, pp. 75–76; *Annual Report of the Maritime Administration for Fiscal Year 1973*, pp. 89–90.

n.a. Not available.

increase from 5.5 percent to 36.5 percent. This increase would be accomplished without taking any cargoes from foreign flag carriers.

These figures are only illustrative and are not intended to show what it would be desirable—or even possible—to do. It is far from clear under what conditions the U.S. merchant marine could capture 80 percent of the annual increase in bulk movements, or whether the massive investment that would be required to do so would be wisely made. These questions are considered in chapters 8 and 9.

The preceding data measure U.S. flag participation in the nation's foreign trade by the weight of cargoes carried. It is just as correct to measure participation by the value of the cargoes. Table 3-3 shows that by either measure U.S. flag vessels carried a much smaller share of the nation's exports and imports in 1971 than they did in 1956, the first year for which both figures are available. But the decline appears more precipitous—and thus perhaps more worrisome—and the level of U.S. participation is lower if the U.S. share is expressed by weight of cargoes carried than by value. The cause of the more rapid decline in the statistics by weight is the considerable growth in U.S. imports of oil and dry bulk commodities in the postwar period, nearly all of which are transported in foreign vessels. On the other hand, the value of these bulk commodities is still much smaller than the value of goods carried in the liner trades, in which U.S. participation is higher.

It should be stressed that the choice is purely arbitrary whether one represents U.S. flag participation in the foreign trades by weight or value. Neither measure is wholly satisfactory by itself. Expressing U.S. participation by the weight of cargoes carried emphasizes the tiny share of bulk cargoes that moves in U.S. vessels. Expressing U.S. participation by the value of cargoes carried emphasizes the larger share of liner cargoes that moves in U.S. vessels. But all too frequently only one statistic is cited: the one that better serves the interests of the speaker. While Congress deliberated the new maritime program in 1970, advocates of the program used cargo statistics expressed in weight to illustrate how much a major expansion of the nation's merchant marine was needed. It was not always made clear that the low level of U.S. flag participation stemmed from the small share of bulk cargoes that U.S. vessels carried. Had this been explained, it might have prompted others to ask how necessary it is that U.S. vessels should participate to an equal degree in all three services— the oil trades, dry bulk trades, and liner trades—and whether the national interest might not be better served by improving performance in the one or two services deemed most vital.

These questions were never raised, at least not in public, and the goal was set of building a merchant fleet capable of carrying 30 percent of the nation's foreign trade, by weight. To reach this goal it was necessary to extend the subsidy program to bulk carriers.

Restrictions on Operators

In return for the privilege of receiving subsidies, contractors must submit to such extensive government supervision over their activities "as to make [the operators] in effect quasi-public corporations."[13] The 1970 act relaxed some of the restrictions, such as one limiting the size of employees' salaries. But others are still in force—many of them in Title VIII of the Merchant Marine Act of 1936. Among other things, they empower the Maritime Administration to examine and audit the contractors' books; they prohibit contractors from owning, chartering, or operating foreign flag vessels, or from operating vessels in the domestic trades; and they require contractors to conduct their subsidized operations in an efficient and economical manner.

One of the restrictions removed in 1970 limited the profits that contractors might earn. This limitation was contained in the "recapture provisions," which operated as a kind of excess profits tax. Whenever a contractor's average annual net profits on subsidized operations exceeded 10 percent of its capital employed in those operations over a ten-year period (a recapture period), the contractor was obliged to pay one-half of the excess to the federal government as a repayment of its operating subsidy (but never more than the subsidy itself). The sums recaptured by the

13. Lawrence, *U.S. Merchant Shipping*, p. 64.

government were formerly sizable, at one time amounting to about 20 percent of the gross operating differential subsidy.[14] During the 1960s, however, few firms earned profits large enough to put them in a recapture
position.

The recapture provisions were repealed in 1970 at the behest of the
Maritime Administration, which argued that they were no longer needed
because the corporation income tax with a current marginal rate of 48
percent performed the same function. This explanation was disingenuous;
for the Maritime Administration must have known that the half of a contractor's excess profits that was not recaptured was already taxed at 48
percent, making the marginal rate of tax on its total excess profits 74 percent. Hence the 1970 legislation greatly reduced the contractors' marginal
rate of tax: from 74 to 48 percent. No one pointed this out, and the recapture provisions were deleted without protest.

Costs of Operating Subsidies

The amounts of money that have been spent in the past for operating
differential subsidies are a matter of public record; hence there is no
special difficulty in identifying the cost of this aid. Figures published by
the Maritime Administration show that from fiscal 1936 through fiscal
1973 over $3.6 billion was paid out in operating subsidies. Most of
these expenditures were made recently. Expenditures before 1955, for
example, were about $226 million—not one-tenth as much as the amount
spent after that date. The low level of earlier expenditures reflects the
impact of the Second World War. Operating subsidy contracts were suspended during the war, and immediately afterward shipping profits were
high, leading to recapture of much of the operating subsidies that were
paid at that time. By the mid-1950s annual expenditures regularly exceeded $100 million; by fiscal 1963 they surpassed $200 million. Since
then their growth has been arrested, largely because of the gradual lay-up
of U.S. passenger vessels, which cost so much to operate.

No major increase in operating subsidies is expected in the future,
only a continuing, gradual growth over time. President Nixon's maritime
program, enacted in 1970, chiefly emphasized the construction of new
vessels for the U.S. fleet, not an expansion of the operating subsidy pro-

14. Ferguson and others, *Economic Value,* p. 53. For a detailed explanation of
how recapture worked, see pp. 51–54.

gram. Nevertheless, some of the new vessels almost surely will need subsidies to compete successfully with foreign flag vessels. Much depends also on how ambitious a program of subsidizing bulk carriers the Maritime Administration embarks on, as well as the state of the world shipping market.[15] On the whole, operating subsidy expenditures will probably continue at the rate of about $250 million a year for at least the next several years.

Passenger Ships

For many years large subsidy payments helped keep in service a sizable fleet of U.S. flag passenger vessels, many of which had also been built with federal subsidies. As recently as 1964 thirty-two passenger and combination cargo-passenger ships still maintained regular sailings. During the next seven years their number declined by twenty-eight, leaving four in operation at the end of January 1971. This remarkable attrition occurred largely for reasons beyond the control of the operators and affecting equally the passenger services of other national lines.[16] The basic cause of the decline of the passenger vessel has been the same everywhere: the development of swift, comfortable aircraft that can offer point-to-point transportation at far lower cost than any ship. For a time it was thought that the salvation of the passenger fleet might be found in the provision of cruising services. The 1936 Merchant Marine Act was amended twice during the 1960s to permit passenger vessels to be withdrawn from their regular trade routes for a part of each year and to offer cruises without losing their subsidies.[17] But most U.S. vessels proved to be ill-suited for

15. The special program of subsidies to U.S. flag vessels to carry grain to the Soviet Union in 1972 and 1973 was expected at first to cost about $50 million (*The Budget of the United States Government, Fiscal Year 1974—Appendix*, p. 260). It has turned out to cost less, in part because American shipowners found employment in other services when the world tanker market improved in 1973, which left fewer ships available to carry grain than authorities had expected.

16. The government of Italy recently announced its intention of gradually ending all long-distance passenger service by the state-subsidized Italian Line, owing to steeply increasing deficits incurred in providing such service (reported in *New York Times*, March 1, 1973). The S.S. *France* has also been withdrawn from regular passenger service, for the same reason (reported in *New York Times*, March 29, 1974; July 9, 1974).

17. By 1972 passenger vessels were no longer required to provide regular service between two points during any part of the year. They could spend all their time cruising and be subsidized while doing so.

cruising, and the few that were not were irretrievably handicapped by the higher costs of U.S. flag operation, even with subsidies.[18] And so even these measures were ineffective; and the fleet dwindled away.[19]

This is not a retrospective account of the U.S. merchant marine, and so there is no point in dwelling further on the decline of the passenger fleet. Its day is over, and only massive infusions of subsidy could have prevented its demise. Perhaps its day was done long ago, and for years only millions of dollars in subsidy payments postponed the closing of this chapter in American maritime history. There is no question of the sizable amounts of subsidy needed to keep these vessels operating. From 1955 through 1970 operating differential subsidy liabilities of nearly $688 million were accrued in support of passenger ship operations.[20] This sum amounts to almost a quarter of all operating subsidy accruals (before recapture) during this period.[21] One vessel, the S.S. *United States,* received $118 million. Despite such large subsidies, a few passenger vessels operated at a loss throughout the 1960s. The last year in which the *United States* earned a profit was 1960.[22] Losses increased later in the decade until they exceeded $4 million in each of the years 1967, 1968, and 1969, when the vessel was at last laid up. The S.S. *Argentina* and S.S. *Brasil* never earned a profit in any year between launching in 1958 and lay-up in 1969.[23] With subsidies other vessels remained profitable until late in the 1960s, when they too began incurring losses and were laid up.

In addition to supporting passenger ship operations with payments of operating differential subsidy, the government was also the source of much of the business these ships received.

In each year since 1962, the Department of Defense Appropriation Act has required that not less than $7.5 million of the funds made available annually

18. At least some of these vessels might have found willing buyers abroad who wanted the ships not for scrap but apparently for use in the U.S. cruising trade. If the vessels were unprofitable in American hands, but promised to be profitable under foreign operation, it must have been the higher costs of U.S. flag operation that explained the difference.

19. The story of the decline of the passenger fleet is told in *Passenger Vessels,* Hearings before the Subcommittee on Merchant Marine and the House Committee on Merchant Marine and Fisheries, 92 Cong. 1 sess. (1971). Additional material appears in U.S. Maritime Administration, Office of Policy and Plans, *U.S. Passenger Fleet: Summary and Prospects* (1973).

20. *Passenger Vessels,* p. 68.

21. For accruals by calendar year, see *Annual Report of the Maritime Administration for Fiscal Year 1973,* p. 86.

22. *Passenger Vessels,* p. 120.

23. Ibid., p. 73.

by that act for travel expenses be expended only for the procurement of commercial passenger sea transportation service on American-flag vessels. The amount expended under this act between 1962 and 1970 on American passenger vessels totaled $70.1 million.

Other agencies of Government similarly supported these vessels, albeit to a lesser magnitude. While statistics are unavailable for all Government-sponsored passengers and U.S. mail, the figures for the *United States* for calendar year 1968 are illustrative.

For that year, the total voyage revenue of $16.9 million (which does not include estimated accrued operating subsidy of $10.5 million) included Government-sponsored passenger revenue of $3.4 million, and $392,000 for U.S. mail. The Government passenger total represented approximately 26 percent of the total number of passengers carried by the *United States*, and approximately 22 percent of total passenger revenue.[24]

That even these payments were in the nature of a subsidy is indicated by the decision of the Department of Defense in 1960 to discontinue sending military dependents abroad by sea and to fly them to their destinations instead. The department presumably took this action for reasons of economy. The effect on the fortunes of the *United States* was both immediate and dramatic. After earning a profit of $1.5 million in 1960, the vessel suffered a loss of $2.4 million in 1961.[25] In 1961 the Defense Department reversed its decision and began sending dependents abroad by sea again; and in 1962 the *United States* lost only $900,000. Other vessels no doubt were similarly affected, though less severely. The department's change of mind must have been prompted by congressional action tying a portion of its appropriation to the purchase of passenger transportation aboard U.S. flag vessels, an action that illustrates again the solicitude that Congress has usually shown for maritime interests. During the rest of the decade Congress repeated this practice to protect the passenger fleet from the department's periodical fits of economy.

And what, it may be wondered, did all these subsidies accomplish for the nation? They postponed the inevitable, certainly. Without these hundreds of millions of dollars of funds, U.S. flag passenger service would almost have ceased before the end of the 1950s. The reprieve these subsidies purchased must have gratified those whose hearts were gladdened by the thought that U.S. passenger ships still sailed the world's oceans. Seldom was a more concrete reason than this offered in congressional hearings for subsidizing the passenger fleet. Supporters of subsidies occa-

24. Statement of assistant secretary of commerce for maritime affairs, in ibid., p. 260.
25. Ibid., p. 120.

sionally argued that the vessels might be needed one day to move large numbers of troops overseas. The Department of Defense answered that argument by saying that its airlift and sealift programs met the nation's defense needs better than a reserve fleet of commercial passenger vessels, and that the cost of keeping such vessels in service outweighed their defense value.[26] The nation's only recent military experience also suggested that the vessels were dispensable, since none were ever required to transport U.S. troops to or from Vietnam.[27]

But even the national security defense argument was usually ignored as champions of the U.S. passenger fleet pressed for remedies that would keep the fleet sailing. The record of the 1971 hearings on passenger ship operations reveals beyond all doubt that the House Committee on Merchant Marine and Fisheries was preoccupied with finding some means of saving the passenger fleet, short of drastically increasing the level of subsidies, and that it never considered whether the fleet *ought to* be saved. The Maritime Administration was more objective and made it clear that it was unable to recommend increases in subsidy of the size that would be needed to keep the fleet in service.[28]

At least some persons must have regarded these subsidies as an advertising expenditure for the nation that bolstered America's image abroad by causing the foremost products of American marine technology to be exhibited to the world. This object has seldom been stated in so many words,[29] but it is certainly latent in the remarks of the most enthusiastic

26. Ibid., p. 303. The under secretary of the navy admitted, however, that "it would be nice to have [the commercial passenger fleet] around provided the [Department of Defense] is not the one to financially maintain its upkeep" (ibid., p. 287).

27. In 1965 nearly half of all U.S. personnel transported to Vietnam traveled by sea, apparently aboard troopships of the Military Sea Transportation Service. The rest traveled by air. This fraction fell sharply later in the 1960s. In 1969 and 1970 no U.S. personnel were carried to Vietnam in ships. (Ibid., p. 288.)

28. The assistant secretary of commerce for maritime affairs testified that at least $87 million in annual operating subsidies would be required to return eight large passenger vessels to operation and restore passenger service aboard four combination cargo-passenger ships—and then only if the maritime unions agreed to substantial reductions in manning (ibid., p. 269).

29. But see the statement in U.S. Department of Commerce, "Maritime Resources for Security and Trade," Final Report of the Maritime Evaluation Committee to the Secretary of Commerce: "Certain intangible values implicit in the national prestige which [U.S. flag passenger] ships reflect must be taken into account. As a leading world power and maritime nation, it is desirable that we have 'blue ribbon' ships carrying our flag in as many trades as possible. Indeed, there is some feeling that our prestige would be seriously damaged if these ships were removed from operation" (U.S. Department of Commerce [1963; processed], p. 87).

proponents of the U.S. merchant marine. If this is a valid objective for subsidy payments, it only adds to the difficulty of deciding whether those spent on passenger operations were worth their cost; for the effectiveness of advertising expenditures is notoriously difficult to evaluate, especially when it is not a product that is being promoted but an organization or idea—or a nation. It might have been possible at one time to use public survey techniques to decide whether subsidizing the U.S. flag passenger service was an effective way of promoting the nation's image abroad. But apparently no such studies were ever carried out, either by the Maritime Administration or by any other group. Now the passenger fleet has gone and there is no longer any point in studying the question.

It might be argued that subsidy payments for passenger ship operations at least created jobs for Americans. So they did—but at an enormous public cost. Take the year 1967, when there were no long strikes to idle ships, and consider employment aboard seven U.S. flag passenger vessels.[30] According to the Maritime Administration there were approximately 3,340 shipboard jobs aboard these vessels. Allowing for normal crew rotation, these jobs furnished full-time employment for about 6,500 men and women. In 1967 operating subsidies to keep these vessels in service totaled nearly $34.6 million.[31] Accordingly, the cost in subsidy exceeded $5,000 per full-time employee, which must have been close to the employees' average annual earnings.[32] In other words, the cost in public funds of keeping people at work aboard these ships was nearly as great as their wages, which suggests that it was not a very efficient method of job creation.

30. The S.S. *Argentina, Brasil, Constitution, Independence, Santa Paula, Santa Rosa,* and *United States.*

31. *Passenger Vessels,* p. 68.

32. One witness stated that the annual payroll for shipboard personnel on these seven vessels, plus four combination cargo-passenger vessels, was nearly $40 million, presumably late in the 1960s when most of the vessels made their last sailings (ibid., p. 6).

CHAPTER FOUR

The Construction Differential Subsidy

THE SECOND IMPORTANT SUBSIDY established by the Merchant Marine Act of 1936 provides financial aid to shipowners for the purchase of new vessels. Several other construction aids are provided by the act, but none has been as costly to the government or worth as much to owners as the construction differential subsidy. As with the operating differential subsidy, "differential" is the key word in defining the purpose; the construction subsidy is intended to equate costs of new merchant vessels built in U.S. shipyards with those of vessels built abroad. It is the differential between the two costs, in other words, that is paid by the subsidy.

The subsidy is only apparently an aid to shipowners. It is in fact a subsidy to U.S. shipbuilders, despite the purely technical feature that until 1970 it was given upon application by the purchaser of the vessel— not the builder. Buyers do not benefit from it, because the subsidy only lowers the price of a new vessel to what the buyer would pay if he ordered the vessel from a foreign shipyard. For many years construction subsidies were paid only for ships ordered by operators holding operating subsidy contracts with the Maritime Administration. These operators were required by law to use U.S.–built vessels, and they understandably regarded the construction subsidy as doing no more than removing a handicap imposed on them by federal law, and shifting to the federal government the cost of maintaining a U.S. shipbuilding capability.

Description of the Subsidy

The 1936 act authorizes the Maritime Administration to accept applications from U.S. citizens "for a construction differential subsidy to aid in the construction of a new vessel to be used in the foreign commerce of the United States." Applications may also be accepted, and subsidies awarded, for the reconstruction of existing vessels; but the act instructs the administration to give preference to new vessels, and that in fact is what it has done.

Since 1970 shipyards as well as buyers can apply for the subsidies. But this probably makes little practical difference, since few shipyards would venture to build a vessel without a strong commitment of interest—or even a firm order—from a prospective buyer. The risk of loss is too great to manufacture ships like automobiles, on the chance that somewhere a buyer may appear who is willing to pay a price that more than covers the builder's costs. Nevertheless the Maritime Administration proposed the 1970 change hoping that it would lead to more efficient—and therefore less expensive—production, and encourage shipyards to apply for subsidies to build large numbers of identical vessels. Previously vessels had been ordered one, two, or three at a time, with each purchaser insisting on differences in design that inhibited builders from producing a uniform version in quantity at decreasing unit cost.

The 1970 legislation amended the Merchant Marine Act to allow the Maritime Administration to award construction subsidies on vessels whose price had been negotiated between the buyer and the shipbuilder. Before 1970 all contracts for the subsidized construction of merchant vessels could only be let after competitive bidding. The following was the usual procedure. After the Maritime Administration approved an application for a subsidy, it solicited competitive bids from U.S. shipbuilders for the vessel's construction. The contract was customarily awarded to the lowest bidder. In the meantime the Maritime Administration had calculated the cost of building the same vessel "in a foreign shipbuilding center." The difference between the foreign cost and the lowest domestic bid was termed the construction differential subsidy. Provided that the price net of subsidy was acceptable to the buyer, contracts were drawn up between the parties. The buyer contracted with the shipbuilder for construction of the vessel and agreed in effect to pay a price equal to the vessel's foreign cost; and the Maritime Administration contracted to pay the shipbuilder the construction differential subsidy.

Since the 1970 legislation, however, nearly all construction subsidies are based on negotiated contracts. Buyers negotiate with shipyards for the vessels they want. After the parties reach agreement they draw up a contract for the vessel's construction. One of the parties, usually the buyer, then applies to the Maritime Administration for a construction differential subsidy. If the application is approved and if the construction subsidy, computed as before, is acceptable to the buyer, the Maritime Administration enters into contracts with the buyer and shipbuilder, and construction begins. As before, the Maritime Administration pays the subsidy directly to the builder. The balance of the vessel's price is paid by the buyer.[1]

How the Subsidy Is Calculated

It is instructive to compare the methods the Maritime Administration uses to compute the operating differential and construction differential subsidies. As explained in chapter 3, the operating subsidy is computed by comparing certain costs of domestic operation with the corresponding costs of foreign operation. The differences are summed up and the total is the subsidy to be paid. In computing the construction differential subsidy, however, the Maritime Administration makes no comparison between shipbuilders' expenses here and abroad. It does estimate the costs of construction in a foreign shipbuilding center, but it makes no similar calculation for domestic shipbuilders. Instead it compares the actual price of a locally built vessel with the apparent cost of building the same vessel abroad and pays the difference as a construction subsidy. If operating subsidies were determined in the same way, operators would set a price upon their product—shipping services—that covered all their costs, the Maritime Administration would compare that price with the estimated cost of providing the same services with foreign labor and materials, and the difference would be paid as an operating subsidy.

The method by which the construction differential subsidy is calculated does not discourage U.S. shipbuilders from combining labor, capital, and

1. Another method of contracting for vessels calls for the Maritime Administration to purchase a vessel from the shipbuilder at the domestic price, then resell it to the operator at the lower foreign cost. After the transactions all parties are left in the same economic position as they would be if they followed the method described in the text. But there is this difference: the Maritime Administration must initially pay the full domestic price from its own account, instead of the smaller construction subsidy, and must therefore ask Congress for a larger budgetary appropriation. The government is no poorer, of course, because it later receives from the ultimate purchaser the difference between the subsidy and the full price. Nevertheless, this payment is not credited to the Maritime Administration's account but is made directly to the Treasury. Hence the Maritime Administration finds itself in the disagreeable position of appearing to be spending more money than it is, an appearance it prefers to avoid by contracting for vessels by the other method.

materials in the most efficient manner possible to produce a vessel that meets the buyer's requirements—unless there were no competition among builders for orders from buyers, for then whatever costs were added by inefficiencies in production would be borne by the government. As long as competition is reasonably effective, however, builders will strive to produce vessels at lowest cost. In practice, of course, competition among U.S. shipbuilders is at best imperfect, but the method by which the construction subsidy is calculated creates no additional costs by biasing producers toward less efficient methods of production.

Operating subsidies, by contrast, undermine incentives to produce shipping services as efficiently as possible, because they cause operators to confront a set of prices for labor and materials that do not reflect the true scarcity value of these resources. This is most dramatically illustrated by shipboard labor, whose price to subsidized operators is only about one-third of its true price. Accordingly operators have much less incentive to economize on the use of labor than they would if its after-subsidy price stood in the same relation to the after-subsidy prices of other factors of production as its before-subsidy price stands to the before-subsidy prices of other factors.

Limits on Subsidy Size

Since its enactment in 1936, the Merchant Marine Act has limited the amount of construction subsidy that may be paid for a single vessel. The limit is expressed as a fraction of the vessel's total domestic cost. At first the act declared that the construction subsidy could not exceed 33⅓ percent of the construction cost. Later the limit was raised as the difference between U.S. and foreign construction costs widened. Between 1960 and 1970 the act allowed the Maritime Administration to award subsidies of up to 55 percent of the vessel's construction cost.[2] During this interval, construction subsidies constantly amounted to about 50 percent of construction costs, and in several cases reached the limit of 55 percent. Thus the U.S. government was investing as much money in the new vessels as the private owners themselves. Not that the owners were always content with the subsidy. Many apparently felt that U.S. shipbuilding costs were well over twice as high as foreign costs and that despite the subsidy

2. From 1962 to 1970, the administration was allowed to award subsidies of up to 60 percent of the cost of reconditioning passenger vessels.

they were still having to pay more for locally built vessels than for similar vessels built abroad.

The maritime legislation in 1970 enacted a declining schedule of upper limits on the amount of construction subsidy that might be awarded on a single vessel between 1970 and 1976. The limit had reverted automatically to 50 percent on June 30, 1970, and there it technically remains. But in testimony before Congress, representatives of the administration stressed that other reforms contained in the legislation would enable U.S. ship-yards to produce vessels more cheaply and so would reduce the difference between shipbuilding costs in this country and abroad. Hence the subsidy should fall too. Beginning in fiscal 1971 the administration expected sub-sidy awards to be less than 45 percent of the U.S. cost of vessels, in fiscal 1972 less than 43 percent, and so forth in decrements of 2 percent an-nually until a target of 35 percent is reached in fiscal 1976. Although these figures have been written into the act, they are not legal limits on the size of awards. That limit remains 50 percent. They are more like productivity goals that shipbuilders are exhorted to aim for; no penalties have been established to enforce their attainment. In the event the goals are exceeded, the Maritime Administration can continue to award con-tracts without disability, as long as the subsidy is not greater than 50 per-cent. Between the enactment of this legislation and mid-1974, however, the productivity goals have been met in every subsidy contract.

The New Construction Program

In 1969 the Maritime Administration proposed to Congress a major program of ship construction for the U.S. merchant marine. The plan called for building 300 vessels over a ten-year period with the aid of con-struction differential subsidies. Maritime interests had urged such a pro-gram for a number of years, claiming that otherwise a large part of the merchant fleet would shortly disappear without replacement. The specter of "block obsolescence" was frequently raised. A majority of the vessels in the U.S. oceangoing merchant fleet had been built during the Second World War and by the late 1960s were approaching the end of their useful lives. Maritime spokesmen argued that without construction differential subsidies most of these ships would not be replaced. Not that construction subsidies could alone assure replacement, since the principal deterrent to American registration is the high cost of operating a ship under the U.S.

flag. This must be offset by some form of government aid—either an operating subsidy or protection from foreign competition—unless the ship is unusually productive, as some newly designed vessels apparently are. Evidently maritime interests took it for granted that operating aids would continue to be given only to ships built in the United States and warned that these ships would be built only if construction differential subsidies were given.

An earlier administration had recognized that there was no reason why operating aids should be given only to vessels built in the United States. The Interagency Maritime Task Force, a group constituted in 1965 to study the government's program of maritime subsidies, recommended that operating aids should be made available to foreign-built vessels of U.S. registry.[3] Two years later the Johnson administration tried to win the agreement of the principal maritime groups to some of the task force's recommendations, including the proposal to allow U.S. operators to buy ships abroad without forfeiting operating assistance, as long as the ships were registered under the U.S. flag. Its efforts were unsuccessful and served only to arouse the anger of the congressional guardians of the maritime industries.[4] The administration apparently judged that its proposals had no chance of enactment, so it never submitted them in the form of a bill to amend the Merchant Marine Act.

The Nixon administration made no effort to admit vessels of foreign construction to the operating subsidy program. Instead it proposed a massive new shipbuilding program to be financed in part with construction subsidies—a program not unlike previous shipbuilding programs except that it is larger. From fiscal 1956 through fiscal 1970, for example, subsidy contracts had been awarded for the construction of 182 new vessels.[5] The new program proposes building 300 vessels (or their "productive equivalent") over a ten-year period. It is expected that much of the new construction will be of bulk carriers, since (as discussed in chapter 3) it is in the bulk trades that U.S. exports and imports are growing fastest and U.S. flag participation is lowest.

3. U.S. Interagency Maritime Task Force, "The Merchant Marine in National Defense and Trade: A Policy and a Program" (1965; processed), passim.
4. The spleen vented on this plan is displayed in *Independent Federal Maritime Administration*, Hearings before the Subcommittee on Merchant Marine of the House Committee on Merchant Marine and Fisheries, 90 Cong. 1 sess. (1967). See especially the exchanges between members of the subcommittee and Secretary of Transportation Alan S. Boyd, pp. 408–74.
5. *Annual Report of the Maritime Administration for Fiscal Year 1970*, p. 23.

No important changes were needed in the Merchant Marine Act to give the Maritime Administration authority to embark on its new construction program. Unlike operating subsidies, construction differential subsidies had for many years been legally available to bulk carriers. Originally they were not. Between 1936 and 1952 vessels could be built with construction subsidies only for use "on [an essential] service, route, or line in the foreign commerce of the United States."[6] This limitation effectively precluded bulk carriers. The reference to essential services, routes, or lines was deleted from the law in 1952 in order that bulk carriers might be built. But none ever were, until the latest construction program began. Funds were scarce throughout this period, and the Maritime Administration used its appropriations sparingly to help build new vessels for the lines holding operating subsidy contracts, which were required by law to replace their ships at regular intervals. This replacement program must have seemed more urgent to the Maritime Administration than the provision of ships to the unsubsidized fleet.

The administration's proposals for a new construction program were received enthusiastically by congressional supporters of the maritime interests, and the Maritime Administration was warmly encouraged to proceed with it. The few changes in law that the administration recommended to expedite the program and reduce its cost (such as allowing shipyards to apply for construction subsidies and establishing productivity goals for shipbuilders) were granted in the Merchant Marine Act of 1970. Most of the ships that have been ordered since 1970 are bulk carriers, unlike the ones built between 1957 and 1970, when only break-bulk vessels serving the liner trades and, latterly, certain novel kinds of vessels also designed for these routes were ordered.[7]

Costs of Construction Subsidies

Like the cost of the operating subsidies, the cost of construction subsidies is disclosed in public documents.[8] From fiscal 1936 through fiscal 1973 the Maritime Administration expended $1,835 million in construc-

6. 49 Stat. 1995.
7. For a classification of orders by type of vessel under the new construction program, see below, p. 126, note 15.
8. The Maritime Administration publishes a historical record of expenditures for operating and construction subsidies in each year's annual report.

tion differential subsidies for the building of new vessels or the rebuilding of old ones.[9] Of this sum $287.9 million was spent between July 1, 1936, and June 30, 1957. In fiscal 1958 another construction program began, and annual expenditures began their climb to a peak of more than $141 million in fiscal 1962. Thereafter they remained below $100 million a year until fiscal 1971.

Spending for construction subsidies is bound to increase during the 1970s as more and more vessels are built under the new construction program. The volume of contracts that have already been let suggests that annual expenditures for construction subsidies will soon exceed those for operating subsidies. During the 1960s they were only half as much. They were $137 million in fiscal 1971, $186 million in fiscal 1973, and judging from the sums recently appropriated by Congress, they will soon approach, or even exceed, $300 million a year.

There is no telling how much the administration's ship construction program will cost by the time it is finished, still more how much the entire maritime program will cost in subsidies and forgone tax receipts. No public estimates of its cost were ever demanded—or volunteered—as the 1970 bill moved toward enactment—apart from an obviously fallacious estimate of $1 billion for ten years offered by the secretary of commerce to the House Committee on Merchant Marine and Fisheries.[10] Newspaper accounts published when President Nixon signed the Merchant Marine Act of 1970 contained estimates ranging from $2.7 billion to $6.0 billion over the ten-year period, the bulk of which would presumably be in the form of construction subsidies.

One reason for uncertainty about future costs is uncertainty about the actual number of vessels to be built. Soon after the program started, officials of the Maritime Administration were speaking of building 300 new vessels "or their productive equivalent." One large vessel may be the productive equivalent of two smaller vessels if their sizes and speeds stand in the right relation. When the Maritime Administration sketched the outlines of its original construction program and determined that the U.S. merchant fleet needed 300 new vessels, it apparently considered building smaller vessels than are commonly being built today. Now it

9. *Annual Report of the Maritime Administration for Fiscal Year 1973*, p. 69.
10. *President's Maritime Program*, Hearings before the Subcommittee on Merchant Marine of the House Committee on Merchant Marine and Fisheries, 91 Cong. 1 sess. (1970), pp. 22–23.

appears that such vessels would be too small to compete with the larger, more productive vessels being built elsewhere. Accordingly construction plans are being revised; larger—and probably fewer—ships will be built.

Not only is the number of vessels to be built uncertain, the kinds of vessels are also uncertain. Costs vary greatly depending on whether super-tankers, ore/bulk/oil carriers, modern containerships, or liquefied natural gas carriers are built. Subsidy rates, as well as total construction costs, vary by type of vessel, hence the cost of the program must also vary depending on what mix of vessels is built.

CHAPTER FIVE

Cabotage Laws

FROM ITS ORIGINAL MEANING of "navigation along the coast," the word "cabotage" has come to denote as well the widespread practice of reserving the trade along a nation's coast to ships of the national fleet.[1] "Coasting trade" is often used synonymously with cabotage in its first sense, and the laws that reserve the trade to national ships are called "coasting laws" or "cabotage laws." In American usage, coasting trade includes not only commerce along the Atlantic and Pacific coasts but also the intercoastal trade (between the two coasts), and trade between the mainland and Alaska, Hawaii, Puerto Rico, and U.S. territories and possessions.

For centuries international law has recognized the sovereign right of every nation to reserve its coasting trade to nationals. Many maritime nations have exercised this right, but none more resolutely than the United States. Cabotage is one of the oldest forms of public assistance to national maritime industries, as well as the most common one among nations. It is the oldest extant form in the United States, and for most of the nation's history was the most important one also. Today its importance has lessened. The decline of the domestic trades in the postwar period has diminished the advantage the maritime industries gain from cabotage compared with what they receive in other forms of government assistance. Nevertheless the costs of cabotage are still large and no study of maritime aids should slight them.

---

1. Cabotage apparently stems from the Spanish *cabo,* cape or promontory. According to one authority, it once meant only navigation along a protected stretch of shore between two capes, whence its meaning grew to include longer coastal voyages that required passage on the open sea.

Evolution of U.S. Cabotage Laws

With few exceptions, limited in time and usually to particular trades, the United States has barred foreign ships from participating in the U.S. coasting trade since the federal government was founded. At first they were excluded through a system of discriminatory tonnage duties. Foreign-built and foreign-owned vessels were taxed 50 cents a ton each time they entered a U.S. port, but vessels built in the United States and belonging to its citizens were charged only 6 cents a ton.[2] Furthermore a U.S. vessel, if engaged in the coasting trade, paid duty just once a year. In 1817 this method of exclusion was supplanted by an express prohibition on the movement of goods between U.S. ports in foreign vessels.[3] An exception allowed such vessels to sail from port to port to unload goods transported from abroad and load goods bound for foreign ports. This statute was the nation's first true cabotage law, and its substance is still preserved in the laws today.

Each maritime accretion to the territory of the United States during the country's expansion was followed by an extension of the coasting laws. After the United States acquired territory on the Pacific coast the inter-coastal trade was reserved to U.S. vessels, marking not only a geographical extension of cabotage but something of an extension in its meaning as well. Soon after the purchase of Alaska, Congress decreed that trade with the new territory should be regulated by the coasting laws.[4] Similar action was taken after the United States annexed Hawaii in 1898 and accepted the cession of Guam, the Philippine Islands, and Puerto Rico from Spain in 1899. It obviously strained the historic meaning of cabotage to assert

2. Act of July 20, 1789, 1 Stat. 27; superseded by the Act of July 20, 1790, 1 Stat. 135, which retained the substance of the earlier statute.

3. Act of March 1, 1817, sec. 4, 3 Stat. 351. Two years before, in an effort to enlarge the trading opportunities open to the U.S. merchant marine, Congress invited other nations to rescind tonnage duties that discriminated against U.S. vessels by offering to reciprocate (Act of March 3, 1815, 3 Stat. 224). Apparently this would have opened the U.S. coasting trade to foreign vessels. Although Congress was willing to share U.S. foreign commerce with the merchant fleets of other nations, it felt more possessive about the country's domestic commerce and so barred foreign vessels from carrying any part of it in 1817.

4. Act of July 27, 1868, sec. 5, 15 Stat. 241.

that it comprehended commerce with a nation's distant possessions; but the Supreme Court interposed no objection,[5] and the coasting laws duly followed the flag to the new colonies.[6]

The cabotage laws of the United States, both past and present, have always reserved the coasting trade to vessels not only documented under U.S. laws but also built in the United States. Originally the first reservation implied the second. Between 1789 (when the first registry law was passed) and 1912, the privilege of U.S. registry was reserved to vessels of domestic construction. The Panama Canal Act of 1912 extended this privilege to foreign-built vessels, as long as they engaged in the foreign trades only.[7] Foreign-built vessels were expressly prohibited from engaging in the coasting trade. This provision has never been repealed and remains a part of the U.S. cabotage laws today.

The cabotage laws were briefly suspended following American entrance into the First World War. With every available ship needed to transport men and supplies across the Atlantic, the U.S. domestic fleet was pressed into wartime service. Congress provided that its place might be taken by foreign vessels, which would be privileged to engage in all the coasting trades except that with Alaska.[8] The suspension was limited to the duration of the war plus 120 days.

Before the period was up the suspension was lifted and the coasting trades were once more reserved to U.S. vessels. Section 27 of the Merchant Marine Act of 1920, which restored the cabotage laws, is familiarly known

5. *Huus* v. *New York & Porto Rico Steamship Co.,* 182 U.S. 392 (1901).

6. But not, as it developed, to the Philippines. The reservation of the Philippine trade to U.S. vessels plainly violated Article IV of the Treaty of Peace with Spain, which bound this country to admit Spanish vessels to ports of the Philippines on the same terms as U.S. vessels for ten years after ratification of the treaty. And so Congress postponed extension of the cabotage laws to the Philippines until 1909, the earliest year the treaty allowed. Before they could take effect, however, the prospect that U.S. tonnage would not be adequate to serve the needs of Philippine commerce caused Congress to reconsider its action and to exempt the trade from the cabotage laws (Act of April 29, 1908, sec. 3, 35 Stat. 70). In 1920 the President was given the power to reserve the trade to U.S. vessels by proclamation; but the power had still not been exercised by the time the islands attained independence in 1946. See Paul M. Zeis, *American Shipping Policy* (Princeton University Press, 1938), pp. 57–58; and Carl E. McDowell and Helen M. Gibbs, *Ocean Transportation* (McGraw-Hill, 1954), p. 92, note 1.

7. Act of August 24, 1912, sec. 5, 37 Stat. 562.

8. Act of October 6, 1917, 40 Stat. 392.

48   BREAD UPON THE WATERS

as the Jones Act, a name that has gained currency as a synonym for all the cabotage laws.[9]

Cabotage Laws Today

The current cabotage laws of the United States are scattered about Title 46 of the U.S. Code. The most explicit reservation of the coasting trade to vessels built in the United States and documented under the U.S. flag derives from the Merchant Marine Act of 1920.[10] The reservation of the trade to vessels of domestic construction is repeated elsewhere in the title.[11] A third section extends the coasting laws to the nation's territories and possessions.[12]

Another section reserves the transport of passengers between ports of the United States to U.S. vessels.[13] This section has been held to be no bar to voyages on foreign vessels that begin and end at the same U.S. port, hence U.S. vessels have no monopoly of the cruising trade. The most recent addition of significance to the cabotage laws is a ban on the landing by foreign vessels of their catch of fish in U.S. ports.[14] Foreign-built dredges are forbidden to dredge in U.S. waters, unless documented as U.S. vessels.[15] Foreign tugs may not tow U.S. vessels or foreign salvors engage in salvaging operations in U.S. waters.[16]

9. But its use in this context is apt to be misleading. The name refers not to an act but to a section of an act; the section did not establish the coastal monopoly but merely reestablished it without essential change after a brief hiatus; the section is still in force but is only one—though perhaps the most important one—of several statutes that comprise the U.S. cabotage laws. To add to the confusion, another section of the same Merchant Marine Act that gave seamen additional rights for the recovery of damages for personal injury caused by the negligence of employers or fellow crew members also bears the name of the Jones Act.

Wesley L. Jones was U.S. Senator from Washington between 1909 and 1932 and an effective representative of maritime interests.

10. 46 U.S.C. 1970 edition, sec. 883.

11. 46 U.S.C. 1970 edition, sec. 11.

12. 46 U.S.C. 1970 edition, sec. 877. The Act of April 16, 1936, 49 Stat. 1207, made an exception for the Virgin Islands. Until the President proclaims otherwise—none has done so yet—trade among the islands and between the islands and other U.S. ports remains open to foreign vessels.

Another exception had been made two years before for American Samoa (Joint Resolution of June 14, 1934, 48 Stat. 963).

13. 46 U.S.C. 1970 edition, sec. 289.

14. Act of September 2, 1950, 64 Stat. 577. 46 U.S.C. 1970 edition, sec. 251.

15. 46 U.S.C. 1970 edition, sec. 292.

16. 46 U.S.C. 1970 edition, sec. 316.

Costs of Cabotage

It is useless to pretend that the full costs of cabotage can ever be determined. In particular, the indirect costs are impossible to reckon. These are the costs that shippers must bear who are forced by the high costs of domestic shipping to send their goods by other forms of transport. How much more must shippers pay to send their goods by truck or rail, or even by air, instead of by sea aboard low-cost foreign carriers? Of course, it is not shippers alone who must pay these costs. Their customers share them, by paying higher prices for the goods they buy. Because prices are higher, customers substitute cheaper goods for dearer ones. In extreme cases entire markets may be lost to certain products. Whether consumers merely curtail their purchases of the dearer goods, or shun the goods entirely, they suffer what economists call a welfare loss when their consumption opportunities are abridged in this way.

There is little that can be done to measure this loss. Perhaps the loss associated with a particular product could be estimated, but there is no practical way of measuring the aggregate loss throughout the economy. That is no reason, however, for overlooking these indirect costs, or for assuming them to be small; they may not be. Nevertheless, in the rest of this discussion these indirect costs are ignored.

Even the direct costs of cabotage are incapable of exact measurement; but at least a rough idea can be formed of their magnitude. Direct costs are the additional costs attributable to the cabotage laws of operating vessels in the U.S. domestic trades. The cabotage laws affect a great many maritime activities, from fishing and salvaging to the operation of tanker fleets along the U.S. coast, but this study focuses solely on the effects of these laws on domestic oceanborne commerce, because these are most readily measured and are likely to be of greatest importance.

Two features of the U.S. cabotage laws must be distinguished: first, the condition that only vessels built in the United States may engage in the domestic trades (called here the building restriction); and second, the reservation of domestic commerce to U.S. flag vessels, with all the attendant expenses that entails (called here the operating restriction). They are quite different restrictions. Their costs have therefore to be estimated separately. In addition, each is of singular interest, since one could be used in a system of protection without the other.

Costs of the Building Restriction

Despite obvious differences in form, the building restriction and the program of construction differential subsidies are essentially similar methods of assisting the shipbuilding industry. Both function alike, by increasing the demand for the products of U.S. shipyards. The building restriction increases demand by barring access to foreign markets: whoever wishes to operate ships in the domestic trades must build his ships in domestic yards. Construction subsidies increase demand by lowering the price of the domestic product. The two forms of assistance are administered through different parties: the building restriction affects demand by operators in the domestic trades; the construction subsidies affect demand by operators in the foreign trades.

The building restriction has greatly increased the cost of acquiring new vessels for the U.S. domestic fleet. Between 1950 and 1970 U.S. customers of American shipyards paid an estimated $900 million to $1 billion more for the construction of new vessels and conversion of old ones than they would have paid for the same work abroad. This sum is not much less than the $1.13 billion of aid given directly to the shipbuilding industry between 1954 and 1970 as construction subsidies.

In recent years construction subsidies have been of substantially greater benefit to shipbuilders than the building restriction. Relatively few large vessels were ordered for private account from U.S. shipyards between 1960 and 1965 without the aid of a construction subsidy. Unsubsidized orders picked up during the second half of the decade; but for all eleven years from 1960 through 1970 just over $1 billion was spent on construction subsidies, compared with estimated costs of $600 million over foreign prices that U.S. shipowners paid for unsubsidized new construction and conversions in domestic shipyards.

In preparing these cost estimates for 1950–70, I assumed that no U.S. shipowner would have built his vessels in the United States or performed conversions here after July 1956[17] without a construction subsidy if the building restriction had not forced him to do so. Once the value of unsubsidized new construction and conversions performed in U.S. shipyards had been determined, an estimate was made of the cost of such work abroad. The difference (modified by one-third as described below) is the

17. It was not until July 14, 1956, that the cabotage laws were amended to exclude from the domestic trades vessels that were built in the United States but subsequently rebuilt abroad.

amount—nearly $1 billion—offered above as an estimate of the cost of the building restriction.

The assumption—unflattering to U.S. shipbuilders—that U.S. shipowners patronized domestic yards only because they had to is certainly extreme and in fact was subsequently modified. During the 1950s a few vessels were built here for foreign registry. The cabotage laws played no role in securing this work for U.S. shipyards. The business must have come here because the price was right or delivery was quick, or for other reasons. This suggests that U.S. shipyards were occasionally able to compete with foreign builders, and that at least some U.S. shipowners would have built their vessels in this country regardless of the building restriction. This must have been especially true immediately after the Suez Canal was closed in 1956, an event that precipitated a flood of orders everywhere for new tonnage. With the world's shipyards working at capacity, a number of vessels were ordered from U.S. yards for foreign registry. Under the circumstances, it is hardly conceivable that all, or perhaps even most, of the unsubsidized vessels built in the United States for U.S. registry in 1958 and 1959 would have been built abroad in the absence of the building restriction. Accordingly, the assumption was amended and the estimate of the cost of the building restriction between 1950 and 1959 was lowered by an arbitrary one-third.

No such adjustment seems necessary for later years. No ships were built for foreign registry in U.S. shipyards during the 1960s, presumably because the domestic product was priced roughly twice as high as the foreign product. It is plausible to suppose that no private shipowner would deliberately have bought so costly a vessel, and that those shipowners who did build in this country without benefit of construction subsidies did so only because of the cabotage laws.

The published rates of the construction differential subsidy were used to compute the cost of comparable foreign-built vessels. For vessels ordered in 1961, for example, the average rate of the construction subsidy on all subsidized contracts awarded in 1961 was used. For years before 1957, when the first postwar construction program began, it was assumed that the subsidy rate would have been 45 percent. In most cases these rates were adjusted before they were used. Until a few years ago nearly all subsidized construction in this country was of break-bulk cargo vessels, whereas nearly all recent unsubsidized construction has been of tankers. The extra cost of building a tanker in this country over the cost of building it abroad, expressed as a fraction of the domestic cost, is ordinarily less than the corresponding increment for a break-bulk vessel. Hence the subsidy rate was lowered by one-tenth (from, say, 45 percent to 40.5 percent) to compute the foreign costs of tankers.

Costs of the Operating Restriction

The costs of the operating restriction are more difficult to estimate. If the cabotage laws were ever repealed, foreign operators presumably would enter U.S. domestic service, compete against each other and against U.S. operators, and by their competition drive shipping rates lower. It is uncertain how low rates would fall, but it is reasonable to expect them to fall by roughly the difference between the costs of U.S. operators and the lower costs of foreign operators.[18] Hence the problem of determining what the costs are of the operating restriction becomes one of determining how much lower the costs would be for foreign operators if they entered the U.S. domestic trades than the current costs of U.S. operators.

Pursuing this approach, I calculate that the costs of the operating restriction must currently total between $100 million and $150 million a year and since 1950 have probably exceeded $2 billion. Both of these figures are lower than the costs of the operating differential subsidy. The domestic oceangoing fleet has shrunk considerably since 1950, but the annual costs of the operating restriction have probably increased in the meantime, owing to the widening difference between the operating costs of U.S. and foreign vessels.[19]

Although prepared with care, these estimates are necessarily based on a number of assumptions and numerical estimates that are themselves somewhat uncertain. The figures should therefore be regarded only as

18. A more sophisticated analysis would recognize that not all U.S. operators have the same costs, nor all foreign operators either, and that under conditions of reasonably free competition prices would fall by the difference between the costs of the current marginal U.S. operator—the one that is just covering costs—and the lower costs of the new marginal operator, U.S. or foreign, after foreign operators had joined the competition. In view of the meager cost data available, there is no point in trying to put flesh on this model. It is difficult enough to determine what the costs are of a representative U.S. operator and its potential foreign competitors, without puzzling over the costs of marginal operators.

19. On December 31, 1950, 453 U.S. flag oceangoing merchant vessels of 1,000 gross tons and over, with a capacity of 5,805,000 deadweight tons, were employed in domestic trade. On July 1, 1974, the corresponding figures were 202 vessels and 5,169,000 deadweight tons. (Data from U.S. Maritime Administration, Office of Subsidy Administration.)

approximations to the true costs of the operating restriction. Despite their faults, however, the figures are accurate enough to indicate that the costs are sizable, even in comparison with the costs of the operating differential subsidy.

The costs reported here were contrived from estimates of the operating costs of U.S. and foreign vessels. Operating costs were in turn estimated from data collected by the Maritime Administration. None of these data were perfectly suitable for the use made of them here. The Maritime Administration collects no cost data from operators in the domestic trades; hence their costs had to be estimated from similar data coming from U.S. operators in the foreign trades. Any errors that spring from this source should be small.

Determining the costs of foreign operators is more troublesome. Of all the world's operators—whose costs vary widely—which ones would enter U.S. domestic service if the cabotage laws were lifted? How would their operating costs change after they entered? Perhaps a painstaking study could answer these questions. Lacking the resources to make such a study, I assumed here that the most successful entrants would come from the principal foreign competitors of U.S. operators on the North Atlantic trade routes and that it would be the difference between their costs and the costs of U.S. operators that would measure possible savings to American customers. The size of this difference was determined with the help of the operating subsidy rates that the Maritime Administration computes for its own purposes. Estimated savings were generally rounded downward so that if they should err they would err on the low side.

It must be assumed that estimates for recent years are the most reliable. Fragmentary cost information was used to prepare estimates of savings in earlier years in order to obtain some idea of the costs of the operating restriction since 1950.

Only operating costs were considered in the calculation because of the difficulty of identifying savings from other sources. To the degree that foreign operators have lower administrative costs, for example, than U.S. operators, the operating restriction has been even more costly than the estimate here of $2 billion since 1950.

CHAPTER SIX

Tax Subsidies
to the Maritime Industries

THE MARITIME INDUSTRIES are the beneficiaries of an extraordinary form of financial assistance given by authorities through the federal tax system. No other industry is granted similar benefits. By creating funds that are protected from tax and depositing earnings into those funds, ship-owners can compel the federal government to share their expenditures for new ships and equipment. To claim this assistance shipowners must make their purchases from U.S. producers, thus conferring a derivative benefit on U.S. shipbuilders in the form of increased demand for the products of their yards.

Until 1970 only subsidized operators were eligible for this assistance. And exceedingly valuable assistance it was: a Treasury Department report in 1951 estimated that the value of the tax benefits that operators received between 1938 and 1949 was greater even than the operating differential subsidies they had been paid.[1] Since then the tax subsidies have declined in importance compared with the operating subsidies. They are still far from negligible, however, and promise to become increasingly important within the next several years as a result of changes written by the Merchant Marine Act of 1970.

The tax subsidies differ in one important respect from the direct maritime subsidies described in previous chapters: their benefits are given in the form of interest-free loans rather than outright expenditures. The program of tax subsidies functions as a loan program, in which the federal government forgoes collecting taxes on a part of shipowners' earnings and grants the owners the use of these taxes on condition that they invest

1. *Scope and Effect of Tax Benefits Provided in the Maritime Industry,* A Report by the Secretary of the Treasury, H. Doc. 213, 82 Cong. 1 sess. (1951); reprinted in *Long Range Shipping Bill,* Hearings before the House Committee on Merchant Marine and Fisheries, 82 Cong. 2 sess. (1952), pp. 45–67.

their earnings in new ships and equipment. Eventually the taxes will have to be paid; but no interest is charged for their use in the meantime—a benefit of considerable value to shipowners.[2]

Capital Construction Funds

The Merchant Marine Act of 1970 authorized U.S. ship operators to establish "capital construction funds," into which they can deposit earnings and other receipts, and from which they can make withdrawals to buy ships and equipment.[3] Capital construction funds closely resemble the "capital reserve funds" that subsidized operators were required to maintain, together with similar "special reserve funds," between 1936 and 1970. The purpose of the capital reserve funds was to ensure that operators systematically saved enough money to replace their aging vessels and renew their fleets. Special reserve funds were intended chiefly to protect the government's contingent interest in an operator's profits, by ensuring that if those profits should exceed 10 percent a year of the operator's invested capital during a recapture period, money would be available to repay a part of the operating subsidy, as required by the recapture provisions.[4] The act of 1970 abolished special reserve funds and deleted from the law all references to them. Capital reserve funds remain, under their new name of capital construction funds, but amended in a number of important ways.

How Tax Subsidies Are Granted

It is easiest to explain how the tax subsidies are granted by first examining procedures before 1970 and then the changes made in that year.[5] Before the 1970 act subsidized operators were required to deposit each

2. The tax subsidies are more complicated to explain than any of the other federal maritime aids. Accordingly readers who are only interested in what these subsidies have cost the public—and not how they are given and measured—may wish to skip ahead to page 66 and the section on the costs of the tax subsidies.

3. Merchant Marine Act of 1970, sec. 21, 84 Stat. 1026, amending the Merchant Marine Act of 1936, sec. 607, 49 Stat. 2005. 46 U.S.C. 1970 edition, sec. 1177.

4. See pages 29–30 on the recapture provisions.

5. The following, somewhat simplified account of how the capital reserve funds worked is taken largely from an internal memorandum prepared by the Maritime Administration and reprinted in part in Gerald R. Jantscher, "Federal Aids to the Maritime Industries," in Joint Economic Committee, *The Economics of Federal*

year in their capital reserve funds the depreciation charges on their subsidized vessels, proceeds from the sale or indemnities for the loss of subsidized vessels, and such other portions of their earnings as the Maritime Administration deemed to be necessary to build up an adequate replacement fund. The earnings on assets already in the funds had to remain in the funds. In addition, operators could make voluntary deposits of earnings with the permission of the Maritime Administration.

The Merchant Marine Act of 1936 stated that deposits of earnings in the operators' reserve funds "shall be exempt from all Federal taxes"; but a disagreement arose after the Second World War between the operators and the Bureau of Internal Revenue over the meaning of this language. As a result a series of closing agreements, or contracts, were negotiated between the bureau and the operators. The agreements provided that beginning in 1946 deposits of ordinary income and capital gains would be treated as tax-deferred rather than tax-exempt, and that a tax on these deposits would eventually be collected through a reduction in the tax base of every vessel bought from the funds. The subsidy was thereby transformed from an outright grant, given in the form of a permanent reduction in taxes, to an interest-free loan, in which beneficiaries were permitted the use of tax moneys for a period of time.[6]

An illustration may help clarify these remarks. Suppose an operator's net income from shipping operations in one year was $5 million before $2 million of depreciation charges on his subsidized vessels was subtracted. Suppose that the operator also sold one of his vessels during the year and realized a capital gain of $500,000. If the federal corporate income tax rate was a flat 48 percent on ordinary corporate income and 30 percent on corporate capital gains, and if the operator made no deposits in his reserve fund, his federal income tax liability would be

---

Subsidy Programs, A Compendium of Papers submitted to the Subcommittee on Priorities and Economy in Government of the Joint Economic Committee, pt. 6, *Transportation Subsidies,* 93 Cong. 1 sess. (1973), pp. 786–87 (Brookings Reprint 263). An excellent summary appears in the statement of Thomas F. Field, executive director of Taxation with Representation, in *The Maritime Program,* Hearings before the Merchant Marine Subcommittee of the Senate Committee on Commerce, 91 Cong. 2 sess. (1970), pp. 615–32. A more complete account, with citations of statutes, court decisions, and administrative regulations, is contained in Richard E. Madigan, *Taxation of the Shipping Industry* (Cornell Maritime Press, 1971), chap. 4.

6. The closing agreements also settled the tax status of earlier deposits in the funds. Some deposits were indeed permanently exempted from tax. For details see Jantscher, "Federal Aids to the Maritime Industries," p. 786.

$1,590,000.[7] Now suppose that the operator deposited in his fund all $2 million of depreciation charges and $500,000 of capital gains, plus $1 million of free earnings. The deposit of depreciation charges has no effect on the operator's tax liability, since these charges were fully deductible anyway from the operator's net income for income tax purposes. Accordingly they are known as tax-paid deposits. Deposits of capital gains and free earnings, on the other hand, reduce the operator's immediate tax liability. In this example the operator would be entitled by his closing agreement to deduct $1 million from his ordinary corporate income and $500,000 from his capital gains in computing taxable income —which would mean an immediate tax saving of $630,000.

Deposits of free earnings and capital gains, as well as all earnings on assets already in the funds, are called tax-deferred deposits because the tax on them has only been postponed, not forgiven. Eventually it will be collected in the following manner. When tax-deferred deposits are withdrawn from a fund and used to purchase a new vessel, the tax base the vessel acquires will be reduced below the purchase price by the amount of the vessel's price that was paid with tax-deferred moneys. If, for example, the operator withdrew $10 million from his capital reserve fund to pay the full price of a new vessel, and if half the $10 million were tax-paid deposits and the other half tax-deferred deposits, the vessel's tax base would be $5 million. In subsequent years the operator could deduct from his earnings depreciation charges amounting to just $5 million (less a small residual value, neglected hereafter) over the life of the vessel, not $10 million. The operator's taxable income during this period should therefore be $5 million greater than it would be if the vessel had been bought entirely with tax-paid moneys. And so, eventually, if tax rates remain the same, the Internal Revenue Service should collect the same taxes from the operator as it would have done earlier if the operator's free earnings had not been put in a tax-protected fund.

In practice, however, the federal government may have longer to wait to collect what is due than this example suggests. For the operator can avoid paying tax on the earnings of the new vessel simply by depositing those earnings in the same reserve fund. Thus in the preceding example it appeared that the government would belatedly collect its tax through a reduction of the depreciation charges that the operator could claim. But suppose that the operator could deposit earnings in his reserve fund in

7. Equal to 48 percent of $3 million plus 30 percent of $500,000.

amounts corresponding to depreciation charges computed on the full purchase price of the vessel, regardless of what part of the price had been paid with tax-deferred moneys. Referring again to the previous example, suppose that the operator could deposit $10 million of earnings in his reserve fund during the life of the vessel, instead of the $5 million that is all the Internal Revenue Service will allow to be written off. Since no tax need be paid on the deposited amounts, the owner succeeds in again postponing the payment of his liability.

This describes exactly what an operator may do. To compute the amounts to be deposited in their capital reserve funds, subsidized operators were required by the Maritime Administration to write off the full purchase price of their vessels over the vessels' lives. To be sure, only the depreciation charges recognized by the Internal Revenue Service ($5 million in the previous example) were tax-paid deposits; the rest were tax-deferred deposits, which the operator must one day pay tax upon. But because this procedure can be repeated again and again, the day of reckoning can be postponed indefinitely.

Changes Made in 1970

The 1970 legislation that renamed capital reserve funds capital construction funds made no important changes in the way the tax benefits are given.[8] Some new terminology has been introduced. The statute now directs that three accounts should be maintained in each capital construction fund: a capital account, a capital gain account, and an ordinary income account. Using the terms employed before, these accounts are simply a means of segregating tax-paid deposits, tax-deferred deposits of capital gains, and tax-deferred deposits of ordinary income, respectively. As before 1970 the most important distinction is between tax-paid and tax-deferred deposits, since it is only through the latter that a subsidy is given. Also as before, the tax is eventually recovered on tax-deferred deposits by a reduction in the depreciable base of new vessels bought with these moneys. But the payment of tax can still be put off indefinitely, no less than before 1970, by reinvesting the new vessel's earnings in the owner's capital construction fund.

8. For more details about the new capital construction funds, including a short legislative history of the 1970 amendments, see David M. Richardson, "Capital Construction Funds Under the Merchant Marine Act," *Tax Law Review,* vol. 29 (Summer 1974), pp. 751–93.

Although the 1970 act made no significant changes in the nature of the funds, it did change many of the conditions affecting their use. As a result the capital construction funds are likely to become a more important source of benefits to the U.S. maritime industries than the capital and special reserve funds have recently been.[9]

The 1970 act extended the privilege of creating these funds to a more numerous class of shipowners. Hitherto only subsidized operators were eligible.[10] Now such funds may be created by any U.S. citizen who owns or leases vessels built and registered in the United States and operating in U.S. commerce or the fisheries of the United States. He may deposit the earnings of all such vessels in his fund. Formerly only the earnings of subsidized ships could be deposited—that is, the earnings of ships engaged in the foreign trades only. Now the owners of ships engaged in the coastwise trades, such as oil companies that operate fleets of tankers to carry petroleum products from Texas to Middle Atlantic refineries, may put the earnings from these vessels in capital construction funds. So may the owners of vessels operating in the noncontiguous domestic trades, serving Alaska, Hawaii, Puerto Rico, and U.S. territories and possessions. The earnings of ships on the Great Lakes may be deposited in the funds, as well as the earnings of U.S. fishing vessels. In short, scarcely any restrictions remain on who may create these funds and what vessels' earnings may be deposited in them. Such liberality is bound to be followed by an increase in their use—and therefore by an increase in the annual cost of the maritime subsidies.

The 1970 amendments do restrict the kinds of vessels that may be built with moneys from the funds. The restrictions were more severe before 1970, when owners could make withdrawals to buy vessels only for service on essential foreign trade routes or for cruising services. Now vessels may be bought with moneys from the funds for operation in the U.S. foreign trades, in the U.S. noncontiguous domestic trades, on the Great Lakes,

9. The maritime administrator said at that time: "It is my opinion that there is no feature of the 1970 act that is in [sic] any more important or in fact compares to [the tax deferral provisions]." *Maritime Authorization—1972; Supplemental—1971,* Hearings before the Subcommittee on Merchant Marine of the House Committee on Merchant Marine and Fisheries, 92 Cong. 1 sess. (1971), p. 24.

10. Unsubsidized operators have been eligible for many years for the more limited tax benefits that are available through the establishment of "construction reserve funds," which are authorized by section 511 of the Merchant Marine Act of 1936. These funds never offered shipowners advantages as large as those that the capital and special reserve funds offered the subsidized operators. Accordingly they are omitted from discussion here.

or in the fisheries of the United States. The only ocean trade that is excluded is the coastwise trade. Thus, although the owners of the tanker fleets that operate between Texas and the Middle Atlantic coast can deposit their receipts in capital construction funds, they cannot use those moneys to build new vessels for operation in that trade. But they can use the funds to build vessels for operation between Alaska and the Pacific coast, a noncontiguous trade.

Owners may also draw upon their funds to buy containers and barges that are built in the United States and are to be part of the complement of a vessel in one of the approved trades. They may use their funds to reconstruct such vessels—and the barges and containers of such vessels—provided they have the work done in an American yard.

Withdrawals for any other purpose (called nonqualified withdrawals) are penalized by requiring the owner of the fund to include the tax-deferred portion of the withdrawn sum in his taxable income in the year of withdrawal. Interest is charged as if the additional tax had been due in the year the amount was deposited. Presumably regulatory safeguards will be developed to prevent shipowners from making nonqualified withdrawals in years when they suffer losses, thereby using these funds to escape paying income tax.

The new language of section 607 is considerably more specific than the old when it touches on such matters as the taxability of deposits in the fund, the purposes for which withdrawals may be made, and the manner in which taxes will be collected on moneys withdrawn from the fund. But on some important matters the new law is silent where the old one was definite. It gives to the shipowner and the Maritime Administration much discretion to decide what conditions will control deposits into and withdrawals from each capital construction fund. Any qualified shipowner who wishes to establish a capital construction fund negotiates his own agreement with the Maritime Administration. In theory, therefore, every fund may be different. For example, the Maritime Administration may require different shipowners to deposit different fractions of their earnings in their funds—and the amounts the Maritime Administration may require are contained within broader limits than they were before.

Furthermore, and more important, it has been left to the agreements, or to the regulations that the Maritime Administration publishes, alone or jointly with the secretary of the treasury, to decide what fraction of deposits that an owner puts in his fund is to constitute deposits of tax-paid earnings or free earnings. In contrast with the pre-1970 law, which required subsidized operators to deposit annually all depreciation charges on their vessels, the new statute establishes no minimum amount that owners must deposit each year. (The statute does fix a maximum amount that owners may deposit that is equal to the sum of all depreciation charges on the owner's vessels, all proceeds from the sale and indemnities for the loss of his vessels, an owner's entire taxable income from the operation of the vessels, and all earnings on amounts already held in the fund—a very generous maximum that in practice is unlikely to be approached.)

Because the statute requires no minimum annual deposit of depreciation charges, there is no way of deciding what fraction of deposits represents depreciation charges and what fraction represents free earnings. To illustrate, suppose an owner deposits $5 million one year in a capital construction fund. Suppose also that he writes down the value of his vessels by $3 million the same year, and that his taxable income that year is $8 million before he subtracts deposits in his fund. How much should the owner subtract from his taxable income? The answer depends on what part of the $5 million deposit represents depreciation charges. At most, such charges may be $3 million; the balance of $2 million is then a deposit of free earnings, and the owner's taxable income is reduced from $8 million to $6 million. Or the entire $5 million deposit may be free earnings, in which case the owner's taxable income is just $3 million. Under the old law, which stipulated that the owner must deposit all $3 million of depreciation charges in a capital reserve fund, the determination was definite: taxable income for the year, in this example, would be $6 million. Under the new law the determination is indefinite.

The Maritime Administration and the Treasury Department have not, by mid-1974, issued permanent regulations that would decide this matter. The interim agreements that the Maritime Administration has concluded with more than one hundred shipowners define only two classes of mandatory deposits: earnings on deposits already in the fund, and proceeds from the sale and indemnities for the loss of any vessels that are covered by the agreements. These deposits are likely to be small in relation to deposits of the owner's earnings. About the latter, the agreements say nothing to indicate what part of them are tax-paid earnings and what part tax-deferred. And so it appears that, for the time being at least, the owners themselves are being allowed to make this determination. Since shipowners, like other businessmen, are disposed to maximize their earnings net of tax, and since they can reduce their current tax liabilities by depositing free earnings in their capital construction funds, it will be small wonder if they declare all the earnings they deposit to be free earnings, and none to be earnings that represent depreciation charges. If so, the cost to the Treasury of these tax-deferral privileges will be considerable.

Tax Reserve Funds and the Investment Tax Credit

Shipowners did forgo one benefit when they used tax reserve funds that they would otherwise have been entitled to. Between 1962 and 1969 business firms could credit a part of the cost of qualified new investment against their federal income tax liabilities. Since ships met the definition of qualified investment, a firm that purchased a new vessel could claim a tax credit of 7 percent of the vessel's cost. Subsidized operators were eligible for the credit to the extent that they paid for their vessels with tax-paid moneys. But no credit was allowed if they made their investments with tax-deferred moneys.[11] If, for example, an operator withdrew $10 million from his reserve fund to buy a new vessel, and if that sum was composed equally of tax-paid and tax-deferred moneys, the shipowner could claim a 7 percent credit only on the expenditure of $5 million of tax-paid moneys.

The denial of the credit decreased the attraction of borrowing from the federal government. If a shipowner borrowed, say, $2.4 million from a bank toward the price of a new merchant vessel, the fact that the money was on loan would not disqualify him from claiming a tax credit of 7 percent of the sum, or $168,000. If the money were borrowed from the government, however, in the form of a deferral of taxes on a deposit of $5 million of free earnings in the operator's reserve fund (assuming the corporate income tax rate was 48 percent), no tax credit could be claimed. What is more, the Internal Revenue Service even asserted that no credit was available on the investment of the after-tax portion of tax-deferred earnings, that is, of the portion of the deposit that was not a loan of public funds. Thus in the preceding example the operator could claim no credit on any part of the $5 million of free earnings that he deposited in his fund and later withdrew to invest in new ships, as if by borrowing $2.4 million from the Treasury the operator had disqualified another $2.6 million of his own money for the investment tax credit.

The companies strongly disagree with the service's position, and in

11. U.S. Internal Revenue Service, *Internal Revenue Bulletin: Cumulative Bulletin 1967-2* (1968), Revenue Ruling 67-395, pp. 11–12.

mid-1974 several were challenging it in court. One case was settled before judgment in 1973 on terms that were not made public, but that reportedly allowed a credit to the operator on the part of his investment made with after-tax funds.[12]

The investment tax credit was reinstated in the law in 1971. It seems probable that, as before, no credit will be allowed on the portion of investments made with public funds on loan to shipowners. Accordingly the costs of the tax-deferral provisions will be somewhat lower than they would otherwise be in the absence of the credit.

Tax Deferral and Tax Exemption

The costs of the maritime tax subsidies raise peculiar problems of measurement, stemming from the form in which the benefits are given. Since the subsidies are given in the form of tax deferral rather than tax exemption, it would be erroneous to identify the costs of the program with the operators' immediate tax savings. The true costs are less than this, because the operators' taxes have not been forgiven but only postponed.

The difference in costs between deferral and exemption can be illustrated as follows: suppose that $10 million of earnings is deposited this year and remains in the funds exactly ten years, and then is withdrawn and taxed all at once. If the tax on the earnings is $4.8 million, and if a discount rate of 6 percent a year is assumed, the cost of the deferral could be expressed as $2.1 million (the difference between $4.8 million and the present value of $4.8 million ten years from now), or $2.7 million less than the cost of tax exemption.

The cost of tax deferral is appreciably less in this example than the cost of tax exemption. It need not be, however: it all depends on the length of time the taxes are deferred and what discount rate is used to calculate present values. The longer the deferral and the higher the discount rate, the closer the cost of deferral approaches that of exemption. If in this example the earnings remain in the funds for twenty years rather than ten and the discount rate is 10 percent a year rather than 6 percent, the cost of deferral increases to $4.1 million, or just $700,000 less than the cost of tax exemption.

12. *Lykes Bros.* v. *United States,* Court of Claims Docket 375-69.

These examples illustrate how the costs of the maritime subsidies might in principle be calculated. Every tax-deferred deposit in the operators' reserve funds causes some immediate saving in operators' taxes, but at a cost of taxes to be paid in the future. If, as in the examples above, one knew when the taxes would eventually be paid, the cost of deferral could be calculated exactly. In practice, however, no one knows when the taxes will be paid, and other ways of measuring these subsidies have to be found.

The simplest alternative is to use the cost of tax exemption as an approximation to the cost of tax deferral. This expedient is justified only under certain conditions: the deferral will last a long period of time and the rate of discount is high. If these conditions are met (as they are in the second example above) the error committed by making this substitution is small.

That is exactly how the costs of the maritime tax subsidies were measured in the 1951 Treasury report.[13] After recording that operators had deposited $62.8 million of tax-deferred earnings in their reserve funds between 1947 and 1949, the report stated that "this 'deferment' [of taxes on deposits of earnings] is tantamount to tax exemption so long as the subsidy continues," and went on to identify the cost of deferral with the immediate tax savings that operators enjoyed, as if the deposits were tax-exempt.[14] The Commerce Department criticized the report for equating deferral with exemption, just as the Senate Committee on Interstate and Foreign Commerce had earlier criticized the comptroller general for expressing a similar opinion; but time has proved the critics wrong. Seen in retrospect, the tax benefits the operators received from the deposits they made between 1947 and 1949 have been virtually those of tax exemption.

The reason is that since those first deposits were made more than twenty years ago, the amount of tax-deferred deposits contained in reserve funds or invested in ships and equipment has grown to nearly $650 million. It is immaterial whether the deposits that were made in 1947 were subsequently invested in new ships, whose tax bases were accordingly reduced, or are still in the reserve funds. If they were invested in ships, the reduction of the ships' bases, and the consequent reduction in operators' depreciation deductions, means that in an accounting sense payment of the deferred taxes has already begun. In an economic sense, however, it has not. The steady growth in accumulated tax-deferred earnings during the

13. *Scope and Effect of Tax Benefits.*
14. Ibid., p. 14.

past twenty-five years indicates that for every dollar of deferred taxes that the government has collected, several additional dollars of taxes have been deferred on new deposits of earnings in operators' reserve funds. Hence there has been no net payment of taxes—only a continuing increase over the years in the amount of taxes that have been postponed. As long as tax-deferred deposits continue to grow, the taxes that were deferred between 1947 and 1949 will remain unpaid.

By 1974 deferral had lasted more than a quarter of a century, and there is no sign yet that the accumulation of tax-deferred earnings will soon diminish. Deferral over as long a period as this is indeed "tantamount to tax exemption," unless the rate of discount is unusually low.

What rate of discount should be used in calculations like these is sometimes difficult to decide. One candidate is the long-term cost of government borrowing, on the ground that the nonpayment of these taxes may have added to the amount of outstanding federal debt. On the other hand, it seems to be common practice now to use for this purpose the opportunity cost of federal investment activities. A 1971 statement proposing new standards for the planning of federal water and land resource projects included a discussion of this opportunity cost.[15] The authors of that report concluded that "the appropriate rate for evaluating Government investment decisions is approximately 10 percent" a year (although they went on to propose that a rate of 7 percent a year should be used in evaluating water resource projects, for reasons of no importance here). If their rate of 10 percent is used to calculate the costs of the maritime tax subsidies, for all intents and purposes the deferral of operators' taxes between 1947 and 1949 has turned out to be about as costly to the government as full tax exemption.

And what of deposits made since 1949? Here the deferral has not been as long. But even if the privilege of depositing tax-deferred earnings were terminated tomorrow, it would take many years before the last deferred taxes on the current accumulation were paid; for payment is made only as ships are depreciated. The first taxes to be paid—again, in an economic sense—would be those that were deferred on the earliest deposits, then those that were deferred on later deposits, and finally those that were deferred on most recent deposits. Therefore, even the taxes on earnings that were put in the funds during the last several years would wind up

15. U.S. Water Resources Council, "Proposed Principles and Standards for Planning Water and Related Land Resources," in *Federal Register,* vol. 36, no. 245 (December 21, 1971), pp. 24166–67.

being deferred for twenty years or longer. And so the conclusion in regard to deposits made before 1950 is also true of later deposits: tax deferral has been nearly as costly to the government as full tax exemption.

Costs of Tax Subsidies

Unpublished data collected by the Maritime Administration disclose that at the end of 1970 $649.3 million of tax-deferred earnings were either contained in operators' reserve funds or invested in ships and equipment. The amount of taxes that these earnings escaped cannot be fixed with precision, because some unknown part of the earnings was of capital gains rather than ordinary corporation income. In 1966, when this fraction was last measured, capital gains composed about a quarter of operators' accumulated tax-deferred earnings, which then totaled $598.0 million. If roughly the same fraction of the current accumulation is capital gains, they were about $165 million at the end of 1970.

There is no record indicating when these earnings were deposited. Marginal rates of corporation income tax varied slightly during this period, which means that the tax that was deferred per dollar of deposits also varied slightly. It seems sufficiently accurate to use a rate of 50 percent to estimate the taxes that were avoided on deposits of ordinary corporation income after 1949, since in only one year thereafter did the tax rate differ from this by more than a few percentage points (in 1950, when it was 42 percent). A rate of 25 percent is used for deposits of capital gains. Because no information is available about deposits made during the Korean War, the excess profits tax that was in force at that time cannot be taken into account.

Since $62.8 million of ordinary corporation income was deposited in operators' funds between 1947 and 1949, plus $150,000 of capital gains,[16] I estimate that about $422 million of ordinary income was deposited after 1949, and $165 million of capital gains. The saving in taxes that operators realized immediately was therefore about $252 million. To this figure must be added a tax saving of $23.8 million on operators' deposits between 1947 and 1949,[17] for a total saving of about $276 million. To be sure, operators will eventually have to pay taxes upon these earnings—unless the law is changed, or the corporation income tax is re-

16. *Scope and Effect of Tax Benefits*, p. 12.
17. Ibid.

placed by another. But for the reasons explained above, the deferral extends over so long a period that it is practically equivalent to full tax exemption. Accordingly the gross cost of the maritime tax subsidies since 1947 has been close to $276 million—say about $250 million.

The gross cost of the tax subsidies since the program began in 1936 is the sum of the costs between 1936 and 1947 and between 1947 and 1970. Costs in the earlier period were estimated to be $99.3 million.[18] Therefore total costs over the past thirty-eight years may be put at approximately $350 million.

The net cost of the tax subsidies equals the gross cost less whatever erosion of tax revenues the government avoided by denying subsidized operators a full tax credit on the investments they made with tax-deferred moneys. To compute the net cost the effect of the subsidies on operators' willingness to invest must be considered. At one extreme, suppose that the subsidies had a very potent effect and that operators would have bought no new ships without them. Then the net cost of the subsidies equals the gross cost, because by accepting the subsidies the operators lost no tax credits that they would otherwise have claimed. But if the subsidies were wholly ineffective and failed to stimulate any additional investment, it means that operators merely substituted funds borrowed from the government for capital raised from private sources, on which a full tax credit could have been claimed; hence in this case the net cost of the subsidies equals the gross cost less a hypothetical tax credit calculated on the full amount of operators' actual investment with tax-deferred funds. No empirical studies have been made that disclose what the effect has actually been, and so the conservative course followed here is to assume that the subsidies had no stimulating effect on investment. Thus the estimate of their net cost that follows is too low if the subsidies really did cause investment to increase.

There are other difficulties also in the way of obtaining net cost from gross cost figures. Some are insoluble, since an answer depends on knowing things that in their nature are unknowable, such as how long the investment tax credit will continue to be available. It would also be desirable to know what is the average time interval between deposit and investment of these tax-deferred earnings in operators' reserve funds, and what is the average life of these investments. If precise answers are impossible, a rough idea of magnitudes is not. Even making quite generous

18. Ibid.

assumptions, it is difficult to imagine how the saving in tax credits could much exceed 10 percent of the gross cost of the subsidies. The estimated net cost of the tax subsidies since 1936 is therefore computed to be between $300 million and $325 million.

The current costs of the tax subsidies can be measured by the value of the deferred taxes on recent deposits in tax reserve funds. From the end of 1965 through 1970 the value of operators' accumulated tax-deferred deposits grew from $559.4 million to $649.3 million, an increase of $89.9 million. Perhaps one-quarter of the increase was of capital gains, and three-quarters was of ordinary corporation income—there is no easy way of telling. If these proportions are roughly correct, operators saved about $38 million on deposits of earnings during the past five years.[19] If it is assumed as before that tax deferral is in this case substantially equivalent to tax exemption, the tax subsidies have recently been costing the federal government close to $8 million a year.

These figures indicate that past costs of the maritime tax subsidies have been relatively high, but that costs recently have been low. This will change. Current costs are bound to increase in the wake of the 1970 legislation. How large they will grow it is impossible to say. Much will depend on conditions that are beyond anyone's power to forecast, such as the state of the shipping business; in prosperous years owners may be expected to make large deposits in their capital construction funds, in lean years smaller deposits. By mid-1974 in addition to the currently subsidized operators, over a hundred shipowners have had applications approved by the Maritime Administration to create and maintain such funds. To get some idea of what their deposits might cost, suppose seventy-five owners deposited an average of $1 million of ordinary corporation income in their funds every year. The immediate cost to the Treasury would be $36 million a year. If the cost of deferral is put as low as three-quarters of this amount, the tax subsidies would increase from $8 million a year to $35 million, assuming that subsidized operators maintained their current level of deposits. This is only an illustration, but on the whole it seems more likely to understate than overstate the increase to be expected in the costs of these subsidies.

19. This figure is the product of the corporation income tax rate of 48 percent on three-quarters of $89.9 million, plus the product of the corporation capital gains tax rate of 25 percent on the balance. There is no point in trying to take account of the various levels of surtax that were in effect during a part of the period in view of the uncertainty about the capital gains fraction.

CHAPTER SEVEN

Cargo Preference

THE CARGO PREFERENCE SYSTEM is the principal form of federal assistance to the U.S. merchant shipping industry. This assistance is given through the cargo preference laws, a group of federal statutes that require that not less than a stated fraction of government cargoes, usually 50 percent, moving by sea in foreign commerce must be carried in U.S. vessels. The term "government cargoes" requires explanation. Each preference law defines the cargoes to which it applies, and it is easier to describe the laws separately than to try to frame a generic definition of preference cargo. In general, however, they are goods in which the federal government has some property interest, or that are moving in commerce as the result of a transaction in which the government played some role.

Preference Cargo in U.S. Foreign Commerce

Preference shipments are currently only a small fraction of all U.S. exports and imports. In the past they were larger. Exact figures are impossible to obtain, but according to one authority preference cargo fell from 8.4 percent by weight of all goods moving in the nation's oceanborne foreign commerce in 1964 to 5.4 percent in 1969 (see Table 7-1). (No figures are available by value.) The decline has continued, and the fraction today is surely less than 5 percent.

Preference cargo is overwhelmingly outbound cargo and is therefore a much larger fraction of U.S. exports than of imports. In 1964, preference exports amounted to 18.6 percent of all U.S. oceanborne exports; in 1969, 12.7 percent.

Although preference shipments are only a small part of the nation's foreign trade, they are a major part of all cargoes that move overseas in U.S. vessels (see Table 7-2). Between 1964 and 1969 they were just over

Table 7-1. Shipments of Preference Cargo
in U.S. Oceanborne Foreign Commerce, 1964–69

Shipments in thousands of long tons

	Total shipments[a]		Preference shipments		Preference shipments as a percentage of total shipments	
Year	Exports	Imports	Exports and imports	Exports	Exports and imports	Exports only	Exports and imports
1964	131,942	169,527	301,469	24,605	25,383	18.6	8.4
1965	131,940	190,951	322,891	23,315	24,311	17.7	7.5
1966	145,484	198,991	344,475	25,484	26,143	17.5	7.6
1967	151,261	191,823	343,084	24,445	24,882	16.2	7.3
1968	154,497	211,397	365,894	23,535	24,000	15.2	6.6
1969	157,158	224,281	391,439	19,957	20,563	12.7	5.4

Source: American Institute of Merchant Shipping, *The Impact of Government-Impelled Cargo on the United States Merchant Marine*, vol. 2, Exhibits submitted to the Maritime Subsidy Board, Maritime Administration, Docket S-244 (1970; processed), exhibits 1, 2, 33, and 34.
a. Except exports to and imports from Canada.

one-half of all such cargo by weight; as a fraction of outbound cargoes only, they were 78.1 percent—a proportion that grew to 83.1 percent in 1969 and that has probably remained over 80 percent ever since.

Carriage by Subsidized Lines

U.S. carriers are not equally dependent on preference cargo. The dependence is least acute for those lines receiving operating differential subsidies. Twelve of the fourteen subsidized lines reported that 35 percent of all the tonnage their ships carried in 1969 was preference cargo. As a fraction of exports only, the figure that year was larger: 54 percent.[1] More interesting, however, than the fractions for the group as a whole are the striking differences in the proportions for individual carriers. Preference cargo moves predominantly along a few trade routes, hence is an unusually large share of the cargo carried by the subsidized lines that serve these routes.

1. All statistics on preference shipments that appear in this section are taken from American Institute of Merchant Shipping, *The Impact of Government-Impelled Cargo on the United States Merchant Marine*, vol. 2, Exhibits submitted to the Maritime Subsidy Board, Maritime Administration, Docket S-244 (1970; processed), hereafter referred to as AIMS, Maritime Subsidy Board Docket S-244.

Table 7-2. Shipments of Preference Cargo on U.S. Ships
in U.S. Oceanborne Foreign Commerce, 1964–69

Shipments in thousands of long tons

	Total U.S. shipments on U.S. ships[a]			Preference shipments on U.S. ships		Preference shipments on U.S. ships as a percentage of total shipments on U.S. ships	
Year	Exports	Imports	Exports and imports	Exports	Exports and imports	Exports only	Exports and imports
1964	20,668	10,059	30,727	14,908	15,407	72.1	50.1
1965	18,044	10,444	28,488	14,221	14,803	78.8	52.0
1966	17,687	10,562	28,249	13,770	14,259	77.9	50.5
1967	18,068	6,962	25,030	14,076	14,371	77.9	57.4
1968	17,952	10,876	28,828	14,313	14,742	79.7	51.1
1969	16,623	8,698	25,321	13,820	14,392	83.1	56.8

Source: Same as Table 7-1.
a. Except exports to and imports from Canada.

A few examples will illustrate how large the differences are. A sizable volume of preference cargo, chiefly military cargo, moved from the United States to the Far East during the second half of the 1960s. Three subsidized lines that operate only between the Pacific coast and the Far East benefited especially from this movement. Of the total cargo each line carried in 1969, 45 percent of one line's cargo, 55 percent of another's, and 58 percent of the third's was preference cargo. As a fraction of outbound shipments only, the figures were 63 percent, 72 percent, and 80 percent respectively.

Another, very large subsidized line that operates between the Gulf coast and Europe, Africa, and the Far East is also an important carrier of preference cargo: 56 percent of all cargo in 1969. Again the figures were higher for outbound cargo: 77 percent of all cargo, and the extraordinary proportions of 94 percent and 83 percent of all cargo bound for the Far East and the Mediterranean respectively.

There are other carriers whose cargo is chiefly drawn from the commercial, nonpreference trade. In general, preference cargo is only a small portion of the goods that move in the liner trades between the United States and South America, South and East Africa, and the northern ports of Europe. Accordingly U.S. lines that serve these trades are not predominantly carriers of preference cargo.

One subsidized line, for example, that operates from the east coast to South and East Africa and to Australia and New Zealand reported that in 1969 just 9 percent of all the cargo it carried was preference cargo. Another line that serves the east coast of South America, South and East Africa, and Scandinavia from the Atlantic coast reported a figure of 17 percent, also for 1969. Preference cargo was less than half of even the outbound cargo on all routes served by the two lines.

These examples are taken from experience of the lines in 1969. Records are also available for 1964, 1966, and 1968. These show much the same pattern, except that preference cargo was generally less in the two earlier years than in 1968 and 1969—both in absolute tonnage and as a fraction of total tonnage carried.

Carriage by Unsubsidized Carriers

Until recently U.S. flag operators that received no operating differential subsidies depended almost entirely on preference cargo. This may be changing. It was an unsubsidized U.S. line that pioneered containerized service between the United States and Europe in the late 1960s and competed successfully with other carriers—both foreign and subsidized domestic—for nonpreference commercial cargoes. No subsidy payments for containerized service on the North Atlantic route have been made since 1971, but U.S. flag operators continue to carry a sizable fraction of all liner cargoes between the United States and Europe. Although no accurate statistics are available, many of the cargoes these unsubsidized lines carry must be commercial nonpreference cargoes.

Despite the success of the container lines, the majority of the unsubsidized fleet continues to draw its trade from the preference market. For example, of all the cargo carried in 1969 by four major unsubsidized lines (no container lines among them), 93 percent by weight was preference cargo. Variations among the carriers in the size of this fraction were slight compared with those among the subsidized lines. One of the four reported that 81 percent of its cargo was preference cargo; another, 98 percent. In some services the lines carried nothing but preference cargo.

U.S. flag tankers and tramps were similarly dependent on preference shipments, particularly the tramps. Preference exports composed 87 percent of the latter's outbound cargo between 1964 and 1969, and over 90 percent in 1968 and 1969 alone. Unlike tankers, which were more successful in booking inbound cargo, these vessels usually returned home nearly empty, and this accentuated their dependence on the preference market.

No one should be surprised that unsubsidized U.S. carriers depend so heavily on preference cargo. Ordinary commercial cargo is largely unavailable to them at the rates they require to cover the high costs of U.S. flag operation. The recent success of the container lines suggests that in some novel services the increased productivity of new U.S. vessels may offset higher operating costs and enable their owners to prosper without subsidy. Nevertheless it is widely accepted that older vessels of conventional design—still in the majority in the U.S. unsubsidized fleet—cannot compete with foreign carriers in world shipping markets.

And so many unsubsidized U.S. carriers are reduced to competing among themselves and with subsidized U.S. lines for cargoes that vessels of other nations are debarred from carrying. Under the circumstances the word "unsubsidized" is seriously misleading. The unsubsidized carriers are the beneficiaries of a system of protection established and enforced by federal law for the advantage of the U.S. merchant marine. It has always been recognized by the maritime community that the cargo preference laws are the vehicle by which an "indirect subsidy" (the term commonly used) is given to carriers that receive no operating differential subsidy. This subsidy is contained in the higher rates that shippers must pay for the carriage of preference cargo in U.S. flag vessels.

Conference Rates and Premium Rates

It is not always obvious that shippers pay higher—or premium—rates for the carriage of preference cargo. Many preference shipments aboard liners are of "conference-rated" commodities, which bear a freight rate that is set by a shipping conference and is invariant with respect to the flag of the vessel carrying the cargo.[2] Hence no premium is paid when the cargo moves aboard a U.S. flag vessel. One should not conclude, how-

2. It is a peculiar feature of the ocean shipping industry that freight rates on many commodities are established by international shipping cartels, called conferences, composed of nominally competitive shipping lines that have joined together to fix freight rates and eliminate price competition. If domestic producers of goods and services engaged in such practices, they would violate the federal antitrust laws. But U.S. shipping lines are expressly permitted by federal law to participate in international conferences and concert with their competitors to set uniform prices. They are forbidden, however, to engage in some of the more flagrant anticompetitive practices that conferences were once notorious for.

ever, that the cargo preference laws have added nothing to shipping costs. If there were no laws reserving cargoes to U.S. carriers, shippers could patronize foreign carriers that were not members of the conference and procure space at lower rates. Shippers may patronize U.S. lines that are outside the conference; but in practice there often are none. Only one or two U.S. flag lines may serve an area, and they may prefer to belong to the conference and take advantage of the high freight rates it sets.[3] Of course there may also be no foreign flag lines outside the conference. In the absence of the cargo preference laws, however, some foreign lines might be tempted to leave the conference and bid for government cargoes by lowering their rates.

Other kinds of cargo are "open-rated," meaning that no rates have been established by conferences for their carriage. These may be cargoes that chiefly move in shipload lots aboard tramp steamers, with the transportation rate determined by contract between the shipper and carrier. Much civilian preference cargo is of this class. In these cases shippers are usually well aware that the rates they are paying are higher than foreign flag carriers would charge. The lower foreign rates are called "world rates," and the difference between the two is the premium that shippers pay for using U.S. flag vessels.

The remarks above contain an assumption that conference rates on preference cargoes are apt to be higher than nonmembers' rates. This assumption is perfectly sound. An abundant literature attests that one of the principal purposes of conferences is to prevent freight rates from falling to levels that they would normally reach if shipping lines were free to cut rates to compete with each other.[4] The difference between confer-

---

3. It used to be the policy of the Maritime Administration to *require* U.S. lines receiving an operating subsidy to belong to the conferences in the trades they served, or at a minimum to charge conference rates. This requirement was rescinded in 1963 (*Discriminatory Ocean Freight Rates and the Balance of Payments,* S. Rept. 1, 89 Cong. 1 sess. [1965], p. 42).

4. John S. McGee put it less cautiously: "History fully demonstrates that the objective of conferences has been to maintain rates above the levels that would otherwise prevail" (McGee, "Ocean Freight Rate Conferences," in Allen R. Ferguson and others, *The Economic Value of the United States Merchant Marine* [Northwestern University, Transportation Center, 1961], p. 348). See this source for corroborative references.

I have no intention here of praising or condemning conferences or deciding whether conferences on balance are beneficial or harmful to the general public. This subject is outside the scope of a book on maritime assistance, unless maritime assistance is defined so broadly that it includes government support of the conference system. Readers who wish to know more about conferences should consult

ence rates and competitive rates owes nothing in this instance to the cargo preference laws, nor is it peculiar to the goods that compose most preference shipments. It reflects instead the power of conferences to set rates appreciably higher than the carriers' marginal costs. Even if the cargo preference laws were repealed, conferences would continue to set rates that exceeded competitive rates.

But would they exceed competitive rates by as much as they do now? There are reasons for thinking they might not—and that therefore a part of the difference between current conference rates and competitive rates ought to be included among the costs of cargo preference. Demand for shipping space for most preference cargoes is widely thought to be less elastic than the demand for space for the same commodities in the non-preference trade, owing to the circumstances in which preference shipments are generated.[5] Much preference cargo that moves aboard liners moves as part of the U.S. foreign assistance program. Shippers of foreign aid cargoes are apt to pay less attention to ocean freight rates than private buyers or sellers of the same goods. As a 1965 congressional report stated, "The traffic will bear almost any rate on [Agency for International Development] exports. For example, if India, with an AID loan agreement, needs tractors it must buy American tractors and the purchase will be made regardless of the level of ocean shipping charges."[6]

Even this feature is not enough, however, to establish that the cargo preference laws raise shipping costs. If the demand for shipping space is highly inelastic, a combination of carriers should not be less willing than a single carrier to take advantage of the fact by charging high freight rates. If conferences act like monopolies in setting freight rates, they presumably set the same high rates on foreign aid shipments as U.S. carriers acting alone would do. To show that the preference laws raise conference rates, it must also be assumed that there exists a sizable movement of the same commodities over the same routes in the nonpreference trade, or

---

the following works (listed in order of increasing detail): Carl E. McDowell and Helen M. Gibbs, *Ocean Transportation* (McGraw-Hill, 1954), pp. 389–99; Wytze Gorter, *United States Shipping Policy* (Harper for the Council on Foreign Relations, 1956), chap. 7; McGee, "Ocean Freight Rate Conferences"; Daniel Marx, Jr., *International Shipping Cartels: A Study of Industrial Self-Regulation by Shipping Conferences* (Princeton University Press, 1953).

5. By elasticity of demand I mean the responsiveness of shippers to changes in freight rates. Demand is highly elastic if small changes in price cause large changes in demand.

6. *Discriminatory Ocean Freight Rates,* S. Rept. 1, p. 36.

that such a movement might exist if freight rates were lower. Suppose, for example, that besides the American tractors and farm vehicles that move to Thailand under foreign assistance agreements other American tractors are shipped to Thailand in private commerce; and suppose further that the demand for shipping space to transport tractors that are purchased privately is considerably more elastic than the demand for shipping space in the preference trade.[7] In that case a conflict might arise within the conference between American carriers wishing to establish high rates on tractors and foreign carriers seeking lower rates. Conference members might agree to discriminate among shippers and charge higher rates to those whose demand is less elastic; but this is often difficult to do.[8] To the extent that it can be done, the difference between the higher conference rates on foreign aid shipments and the lower conference rates on shipments of the same goods in the nonpreference trade cannot be attributed to the cargo preference laws. Conferences presumably would wish to establish such rate differentials even if all members were eligible to carry the cargoes that are now reserved to U.S. carriers. If such discrimination is not practicable, however, the carriers have no choice but to decide on a single conference rate.

Since the internal affairs of conferences are conducted in secrecy, little can be said about the bargaining that must take place among the carriers. No doubt they often compromise and establish an intermediate rate. Whether this rate is higher or lower than the rate that would be set without the cargo preference laws it is impossible to say.[9] But the American bargaining position is likely to be stronger than that of the foreign carriers, since U.S. carriers can leave the conference and still retain the preference trade. Their threat to do so should often persuade foreign carriers to agree to higher rates. Only when the high rates threaten to strangle private trade and cause the foreign carriers much harm would one expect the carriers to resist strongly.

Occasionally the U.S. carriers and foreign carriers may not be able

7. As it presumably is if shipping costs compose a large part of the landed cost of tractors in Thailand, and if buyers in Thailand are free to purchase tractors elsewhere in the world.

8. See the discussion of discrimination among shippers in McGee, "Ocean Freight Rate Conferences," pp. 360–61.

9. If there were no cargo preference laws the U.S. carriers would have less reason to press for high rates. On the other hand the foreign carriers would have more reason. Would the result be different? There is no way of telling.

to resolve their differences. The conference may then come apart. Something of this sort seems to have happened in 1960 when

... foreign-flag lines serving the Persian Gulf broke away from the Persian Gulf Outward Freight Conference. The remaining members of the conference are American. The foreign lines left the conference after a dispute over the level of freight rates, which they contended were too high to move commercial cargo. The American lines, on the other hand, refused to lower rates primarily because they were not carrying commercial cargo but AID and Defense Department cargoes. Since conference agreements provide that all shippers are entitled to the same rate, conferences cannot charge different rates to different shippers. The American-flag lines, under the preference laws, could charge high rates and still procure cargo to the Persian Gulf since the Government paid the freight charges. The foreign lines, on the other hand, could not ship these same commodities to the Persian Gulf on a commercial basis at such high rates.[10]

These remarks should explain why a full accounting of cargo preference costs must include a portion of the costs of shipping conference-rated cargoes aboard conference liners. The preference laws increase shipping costs by conferring principal rights of carriage upon a small group of operators, enabling them to price their services much as monopolists would do. The point should not be exaggerated; it would be foolish to contend that there are no restraints whatever upon the freight rates that U.S. operators may charge. Assuredly there are, sometimes economic, sometimes legal in nature. But it would be just as naive to suppose that freight rates on preference goods are competitively established, and that they approximate the rates that would be set if the preference laws were repealed and the transport of these goods were open to all carriers.

It is chiefly shipping costs aboard liners that is of concern here. Because in so many trades only a few U.S. lines are active, they should often be able to agree upon rates in excess of those that would normally be set in a competitive market. The convenience of the conference system is that it affords U.S. carriers an approved meeting place in which to fix rates. It also binds foreign carriers to offer the same rates, thereby creating the impression that the U.S. rates are not unusually high. The carriage of bulk commodities in the tramp trades is more competitive. Accordingly there is less reason to believe that the costs of shipping preference commodities aboard tramp carriers are inflated in quite the same way as shipping costs in the liner trades.

10. *Discriminatory Ocean Freight Rates,* S. Rept. 1, pp. 37–38.

Cargo Preference Laws

Although there exist a number of separate cargo preference laws, including some that were simply provisions in acts establishing foreign assistance programs, three preference laws are of primary importance today and affect nearly all cargoes that are subject to the preference laws.

Military Transportation Act of 1904

The oldest current preference law is the Military Transportation Act of 1904.[11] It directs that all supplies for the U.S. armed services that move by sea must be carried either in vessels of U.S. registry or in vessels owned by the United States. Exceptions are allowed only when the freight charged by U.S. vessels is "excessive or otherwise unreasonable." Although the statute affords no warrant for the practice, the Defense Department occasionally engages foreign vessels to move its supplies when U.S. vessels are not available.

Public Resolution No. 17, 1934

Public Resolution No. 17 of the Seventy-third Congress, approved in March 1934, declared it to be "the sense of Congress" that whenever loans were made by any agency of the government to foster the export of U.S. products, those products should be carried exclusively in vessels of the United States.[12] Although the resolution technically may not have the force of law, it is treated in practice as imposing a legal requirement that at least one-half of the exports to which it applies must be carried in U.S. bottoms.

Public Resolution 17, or P.R. 17, is the least important of the three principal cargo preference laws, and affects only exports that are financed by the Export-Import Bank of the United States. If P.R. 17 were honored

11. Act of April 28, 1904, 33 Stat. 518. 10 U.S.C. 1970 edition, sec. 2631.
12. Joint Resolution of March 26, 1934, 48 Stat. 500. 15 U.S.C. 1970 edition, sec. 616(a). Soon after this resolution was approved, a question arose whether it laid down an absolute requirement that products that come within its scope must in all cases be carried in U.S. bottoms. The attorney general expressed the opinion that Congress did not intend to make the resolution mandatory; that Congress intended only "to lay down a rule of guidance" to be followed whenever it was feasible to do so. (*Official Opinions of the Attorneys General of the United States,* vol. 37 [1936], p. 546.)

to the letter all shipments financed by the Export-Import Bank would have to be carried in U.S. vessels. Usually this requirement is waived, however, and foreign flag vessels are permitted to carry up to one-half of such exports.[13]

Cargo Preference Act of 1954

During the postwar period Congress enacted a number of programs providing military and economic assistance to friendly countries overseas. Several of the acts establishing these programs contained cargo preference provisions that reserved to U.S. ships the carriage of at least part of the cargoes to be moved abroad.[14] These provisions were largely superseded by an inclusive preference law enacted in 1954 as an amendment to the Merchant Marine Act of 1936.[15]

13. The practice of waiving the requirement apparently began soon after the Second World War, when the Export-Import Bank was involved in efforts to help rebuild the economies of war-damaged countries. Some of these countries had merchant fleets that they were eager to employ carrying goods from the United States. The bank understood that if it insisted that all the exports it financed should be carried in U.S. bottoms, it would in effect be taking back with one hand part of what it had given with the other. The recipient nation would be forced to spend scarce dollars on carriage costs when its own merchant fleet could do the job instead. And so, in cooperation with the Maritime Administration, a policy was established of permitting ships of the recipient nation to participate in the carriage of bank-financed exports, provided that the same nation agreed not to discriminate against U.S. vessels in its foreign commerce.

This policy continues to the present day. Foreign recipients of export credits may apply to the Maritime Administration for a waiver, and if their nation practices no discrimination against U.S. vessels in its foreign trade a "general waiver" will customarily be granted. Its terms provide that as much as 50 percent of the goods whose purchase the bank is financing may be carried aboard ships of the borrower's national merchant marine. The rest must be carried by U.S. vessels.

"Statutory waivers" are also granted occasionally. These are authorized by P.R.17 itself, in which the requirement that U.S. vessels must be employed is qualified by the condition: "unless . . . vessels of the United States are not available in sufficient numbers, or in sufficient tonnage capacity, or on necessary sailing schedule, or at reasonable rates." If the borrower can convince the Maritime Administration that one of these conditions has been met, the agency will approve a waiver and permit the goods to move aboard a foreign flag carrier.

14. For a list of these acts, see Earl W. Clark, Hoyt S. Haddock, and Stanley J. Volens, *The U.S. Merchant Marine Today: Sunrise or Sunset?* (Washington, D.C.: Labor-Management Maritime Committee, 1970), p. 53.

15. Act of August 26, 1954, 68 Stat. 832, which added new subsection 901(b), Merchant Marine Act, 1936. 46 U.S.C. 1970 edition, sec. 1241(b). This statute is also known as the 50-50 Law, Public Law 664, and the Chief Cargo Preference Act.

The act covers three classes of goods: goods bought by the government for its own account; goods provided by the government for the account of any foreign nation, if no provision is made for reimbursement; and goods for which the government has advanced funds, granted credits, or guaranteed the convertibility of foreign currencies.

The statute directs that whenever such goods are moved by sea, at least 50 percent of the shipments, by gross tonnage, must be carried in privately owned U.S. flag commercial vessels, provided such vessels are available at fair and reasonable rates.[16] A few minor cargoes are expressly exempted. The act provides that its requirements may be waived whenever Congress, the President, or the secretary of defense declares that an emergency exists justifying such a waiver. No such emergency has yet occurred.

The Cargo Preference Act of 1954 is far more inclusive than the other two preference laws and in fact overlaps them. For example, the Defense Department acknowledges that supplies shipped by sea for the U.S. armed services are subject to the Cargo Preference Act of 1954 as well as to the Military Transportation Act of 1904. Although the earlier act requires that *all* military supplies must be shipped aboard U.S. flag vessels, it does not require any part of those shipments to travel aboard *privately owned* vessels. The 1904 law would be satisfied even if military cargoes moved exclusively in ships owned by the U.S. government. The Defense Department owns its own fleet of cargo ships, which are operated by the Military Sealift Command (until 1970, the Military Sea Transportation Service) of the U.S. Navy. The Maritime Administration holds title to vessels in the National Defense Reserve Fleet. None of these vessels answers the description of a privately owned U.S. flag commercial vessel. Hence they may carry no more than 50 percent of military cargoes, or of any other cargoes subject to the 1954 Cargo Preference Act.

Costs of the Cargo Preference Laws

The rest of the chapter addresses the important question of how much the cargo preference laws have added to the prices that public agencies

16. An amendment in 1961 to the 1936 act added the requirement that the U.S. flag vessels must have been built in the United States or if built abroad must have been documented under U.S. registry for three years. Act of September 21, 1961, 75 Stat. 565.

have paid for ocean transportation. Apart from estimates that Lawrence prepared for shipments in 1962, no estimates of this quantity have been made before.[17] It is probably impossible to be highly accurate, because the data that are needed must be laboriously assembled from sources in several government agencies, not all of which have maintained useful and accessible records. In the past no central agency was responsible for administering the cargo preference laws. This was changed by the Merchant Marine Act of 1970,[18] which empowered the Maritime Administration to regulate how other agencies should comply with the Cargo Preference Act of 1954. The Maritime Administration has already begun receiving information from all government agencies except the Defense Department about shipments of preference cargo that move under their administration. Provided that the Defense Department eventually furnishes the same information, it should become possible to determine what volume of cargo moves under these laws each year, what payments are made for its carriage, and how those payments are divided between U.S. and foreign carriers. But the historical estimates that appear in the following sections are considerably less certain, based as they are on the incomplete data assembled separately by each agency.

The task of estimating how much the preference laws have increased shipping costs is manageable only because just three government activities account for all but a very few preference shipments. The largest volume of preference cargo is generated by the Department of Defense, which must ship millions of tons of supplies each year to U.S. forces overseas. Large amounts of preference cargo are also shipped under the Food for Peace program, as well as under the foreign aid programs administered by the Agency for International Development.

Military Cargoes

No customer buys more shipping space aboard U.S. flag vessels, or makes larger payments to U.S. operators, than the Department of Defense. This may seem surprising since the department operates its own fleet of

17. Samuel A. Lawrence, *United States Merchant Shipping Policies and Politics* (Brookings Institution, 1966), pp. 207–08, 364.
18. 84 Stat. 1018.

government-owned dry cargo ships and tankers, which it keeps continuously employed supplying American forces overseas. But the government-owned fleet is not nearly large enough to furnish the Defense Department with all the shipping it needs. Accordingly the department is a heavy buyer of shipping space from private operators, almost exclusively U.S. flag operators.

THE NUCLEUS FLEET. With the exception of an undisclosed but probably small volume of cargo that is carried in regular Navy ships, all Defense Department cargoes that move by sea do so under arrangements made by the Military Sealift Command, the department's shipping agency. Although this command is a unit of the Navy, and is staffed in part by Navy personnel, its job is to furnish ocean transportation services to the entire Department of Defense and occasionally other government organizations.[19] The command operates a fleet of government-owned vessels, all of which are technically in the custody of the Navy, but only a few of which are commissioned vessels crewed by Navy officers and men. Most of this fleet is manned by civilian crews in the employ of the government. A smaller number of other government-owned ships that have been assigned to the Military Sealift Command are operated for it by private contractors on a cost-plus-fixed-fee basis. Together these ships compose the command's "nucleus fleet."

On June 30, 1972, the nucleus fleet consisted of ninety-seven dry cargo ships, transports, and tankers. It was smaller during the 1950s, but somewhat larger in the early 1960s.[20] It expanded during the Vietnam buildup to a peak of 134 vessels between May 1967 and February 1968 before declining again. Despite its smaller size in 1972, the nucleus fleet still constituted a sizable fraction of the entire U.S. oceangoing merchant fleet, which numbered 655 active or temporarily inactive vessels on June 30, 1972. By comparison, the eleven U.S. liner companies that held operating

19. Other government organizations that the Military Sealift Command has served include the Agency for International Development, the National Aeronautics and Space Administration, and the General Services Administration. It also helped carry United Nations troops to the Congo early in the 1960s.

20. U.S. Navy, Military Sealift Command, *Financial and Statistical Report,* pts. 1 and 2, published quarterly. The nucleus fleet also contained thirty-five special project vessels, such as vessels equipped for oceanographic research that were operated by the command for the Naval Oceanographic Office and missile-tracking ships operated for the National Aeronautics and Space Administration. These highly specialized ships are of no importance in a study of the U.S. oceangoing merchant marine and have been omitted from all statistics in this section.

subsidy contracts with the Maritime Administration had 201 vessels in subsidized service on June 30, 1972.

The size of the nucleus fleet was limited in 1954 by an agreement between the secretaries of defense and commerce, the so-called Wilson-Weeks agreement.[21] Except under conditions of full mobilization, the nucleus fleet must not contain more than fifty-six transports, thirty-four cargo ships, and sixty-one tankers.

The same agreement sets forth the order in which the Defense Department may turn to other sources for shipping space. First, it must make as much use as possible of U.S. liner services. If it needs more space, the department may charter U.S. flag vessels from private owners. If still more space is needed, the Maritime Administration may break out vessels from the National Defense Reserve Fleet and put them in service for the Defense Department. Only after these sources have been exhausted may the department engage space aboard foreign flag vessels.[22]

EFFECT OF THE WILSON-WEEKS AGREEMENT. The substance of the 1954 agreement must be counted among the most valuable favors that the federal government ever conferred on the U.S. shipping industry. By a stroke of the pen the government renounced all intention of operating a fleet of publicly owned vessels that would deprive the privately owned merchant marine of a sizable share of this nation's defense cargoes. It is impossible to say with any precision what this benefit has been worth to the maritime industries. Much depends on how large a nucleus fleet the Defense Department would otherwise maintain, and what use it would make of vessels from the reserve fleet. Agreement or no, some military cargoes would always move in U.S. flag liners, since there would always be times when it would be unthrifty to divert a government-owned vessel to pick up cargoes that a commercial liner was available to carry. Still,

21. Charles E. Wilson was secretary of defense and Sinclair Weeks secretary of commerce for several years during the Eisenhower administration. The text of their agreement was reprinted in *Cargo for American Ships,* Hearings before the Subcommittee on Merchant Marine of the House Committee on Merchant Marine and Fisheries, 92 Cong. 1 sess. (1972), pt. 1, pp. 308–10.

22. The Defense Department is allowed some flexibility in observing these priorities. A literal interpretation of the agreement would forbid the use of foreign flag shipping as long as one serviceable vessel remained in the reserve fleet. In practice it would often be a reckless waste of money to activate a vessel solely to carry a small quantity of cargo that could conveniently be moved aboard a foreign flag carrier. And so the command has occasionally engaged foreign shipping although at no time since the Second World War have all the vessels in the reserve fleet been placed in service.

Table 7-3. Shipments of Dry Cargo and Petroleum by Military Sealift Command, Fiscal Years 1952–72

| | Dry cargo shipments | | | | | Petroleum shipments | | | | |
| | Aboard government-owned vessels | | Aboard privately owned vessels | | Total aboard all vessels, | Aboard government-owned vessels | | Aboard privately owned vessels | | Total aboard all vessels, |
Fiscal year	Millions of measurement ton-miles	Percentage of total	Millions of measurement ton-miles	Percentage of total	millions of measurement ton-miles	Millions of long ton-miles	Percentage of total	Millions of long ton-miles	Percentage of total	millions of long ton-miles
1952	13,480	13.7	85,156	86.3	98,636	34,202	63.4	19,767	36.6	53,969
1953	43,200	39.3	66,709	60.7	109,909	32,655	47.1	36,633	52.9	69,288
1954	27,972	33.5	55,585	66.5	83,557	32,919	55.3	26,574	44.7	59,493
1955	19,111	34.5	36,246	65.5	55,357	21,205	43.7	27,348	56.3	48,553
1956	19,206	35.4	35,026	64.6	54,232	20,971	47.5	23,199	52.5	44,170
1957	16,082	30.9	35,970	69.1	52,052	42,706	74.9	14,315	25.1	57,021
1958	14,376	29.4	34,556	70.6	48,932	25,576	53.3	22,384	46.7	47,960
1959	12,036	24.7	36,629	75.3	48,665	20,701	39.2	32,140	60.8	52,841
1960	11,621	26.9	31,554	73.1	43,175	13,834	32.1	29,309	67.9	43,143
1961	12,057	28.6	30,072	71.4	42,129	14,178	27.9	36,680	72.1	50,858
1962	11,641	22.7	39,559	77.3	51,200	13,883	25.1	41,461	74.9	55,344
1963	10,489	20.4	41,009	79.6	51,498	14,014	24.7	42,616	75.3	56,630
1964	11,465	20.4	44,685	79.6	56,150	13,521	23.7	43,540	76.3	57,061
1965	11,087	19.5	45,716	80.5	56,803	14,524	24.5	44,774	75.5	59,298
1966	25,788	24.1	81,049	75.9	106,837	13,508	17.6	63,200	82.4	76,708
1967	45,613	30.9	101,934	69.1	147,547	13,381	13.3	87,184	86.7	100,565
1968	46,124	28.9	113,499	71.7	159,623	13,658	11.2	108,623	88.8	122,281
1969	39,257	24.4	121,889	75.6	161,146	13,196	12.4	93,064	87.6	106,260
1970	15,493	12.0	114,036	88.0	129,529	12,796	17.3	61,073	82.7	73,869
1971	7,220	7.4	89,899	92.6	97,119	12,083	19.6	49,504	80.4	61,587
1972	7,045	8.3	77,406	91.7	84,451	11,362	18.3	50,558	81.7	61,920

Source: U. S. Navy, Military Sealift Command, *Financial and Statistical Report*, pts. 1 and 2, published quarterly.

the agreement has no doubt increased the volume of military shipments aboard privately owned U.S. flag vessels and inhibited the maintenance of a larger nucleus fleet.

It is no answer to these remarks to point out that the present nucleus fleet is rather smaller than the limits contained in the agreement, and that therefore the agreement can hardly be said to constrain the fleet's size. Quite apart from the fact that no one could sensibly expect the Defense Department to maintain a fleet exactly as large as it is permitted to do, the agreement has also been interpreted as expressing a philosophy that military cargoes should move aboard privately owned vessels to the maximum extent practicable. It has, for example, emboldened berth line operators to press the Military Sealift Command to use commercial liners at every opportunity, even at the cost of leaving some of the command's chartered capacity idle, on the grounds that the order of priorities in the 1954 agreement dictates such a preference. The MSC has resisted this pressure, emphasizing how wasteful it would be not to make the fullest use possible of its chartered vessels during their period of hire. Nevertheless, it would be unreasonable to suppose that this pressure has had no effect whatsoever and that it has not caused the command to make somewhat more use of liner services than it would otherwise have done.

EFFECT OF THE CARGO PREFERENCE ACT. Less than two months after the Wilson-Weeks agreement was concluded, the Cargo Preference Act of 1954 was signed into law. Like the agreement, the Cargo Preference Act had an important effect on the division of military cargoes between privately owned and government-owned U.S. flag vessels. Ships of the nucleus fleet and National Defense Reserve Fleet were implicitly forbidden to carry more than half of all military cargoes. The agreement and the act neatly complemented one another: the one imposed a ceiling on the size of the nucleus fleet and enjoined the Defense Department from using ships of the reserve fleet as long as private shipping was available; the other required that at least half of all military cargoes should be transported in privately owned vessels. It was a jubilee year for the U.S. merchant marine.

In recent years the Defense Department has amply fulfilled the requirements of the 1954 act. Table 7-3 indicates that privately owned U.S. flag vessels carried the bulk of all military shipments between fiscal 1952 and fiscal 1972. Movements are expressed not in terms of the tonnage of cargo lifted but as the product of the tonnage of cargo and the distance it was carried—measurement ton-miles in the case of dry cargo, long ton-miles in the case of petroleum.[23] This is the most suitable way of measuring the shares of cargo moved by different carriers; for if one of two ships that both lifted 10,000 tons of cargo carried its cargo 5,000 miles, and the other carried its cargo 1,000 miles, it would be misleading to suggest that both ships participated equally in the total movement of 20,000 tons.[24]

In all but two years during the 1960s, government-owned vessels carried between 20 percent and 30 percent of all MSC dry cargoes. Their share briefly exceeded 30 percent in fiscal 1967, when more than 170 GAA vessels were pressed into service to help meet the demand for additional shipping to Vietnam.[25] As these ships were returned to the reserve fleet their place was taken by privately owned vessels, and the share of dry cargoes carried by government-owned vessels fell. In fiscal 1972 government-owned vessels carried less than 10 percent of all MSC dry cargoes.

Petroleum is also carried chiefly aboard privately owned vessels. Over 80 percent of the command's shipments of petroleum have moved in privately owned bottoms each fiscal year since 1966.

The Military Sealift Command publishes no statistics of its cargo shipments aboard foreign flag vessels. Hence there is no way of telling what fraction of the cargoes that were moved by privately owned vessels was moved by U.S. flag vessels and what fraction by foreign flag vessels. According to the command, however, foreign flag carryings have never been large. Somewhat meager statistics that were gathered from the command's

23. The Military Sealift Command reports its shipment of dry cargo in measurement tons—a unit of cubic volume equal to 40 cubic feet—but its shipments of petroleum in long tons of 2,240 pounds each. Sometimes statistics in measurement tons are converted to statistics in long tons, by means of tables of conversion factors that depend on the density of each cargo. There is no way of accomplishing this conversion, however, after the statistics for a diverse group of cargoes have been aggregated, as they are in the MSC publications. Hence movements of dry cargo and petroleum are recorded separately in Table 7-3.

24. Nevertheless the 1954 Cargo Preference Act requires only that 50 percent of the tonnage of military cargoes must be carried in privately owned vessels, not that 50 percent of all the ton-miles of military shipments must be generated in such ships.

25. All of the vessels that were broken out of reserve during the Vietnam War were placed under control of the Military Sealift Command. Instead of being manned with government crews, they were operated for the command by private U.S. shipping companies under cost-plus-fixed-fee contracts called General Agency Agreements, whence they were known as GAA vessels.

records for a 1970 hearing before the Maritime Subsidy Board support this statement. They show that in none of the four years 1964, 1966, 1968, and 1969 did foreign flag vessels carry as much as 1 percent of the volume of MSC dry cargoes that were lifted by liners to foreign destinations from the United States.[26] These figures cover only a limited portion of all shipments by the Military Sealift Command—petroleum shipments are excluded, for example, and so are all shipments that originated abroad— but within their compass they do confirm that foreign carriers participated very little in the carriage of U.S. military cargoes.

From fiscal 1952, the earliest year for which figures are available, through fiscal 1972, the Military Sealift Command has spent more than $8.6 billion to procure shipping space aboard privately owned vessels. Much of this sum was paid for space aboard liners; the balance was paid for the charter of vessels.[27] Almost all the space that the command purchased was aboard U.S. flag vessels, as required by the cargo preference laws.

COST TO MSC. How much money might have been saved had the command been allowed to patronize foreign flag carriers? The estimates presented here suggest that the preference laws must have cost the command at least several billion dollars over the past two decades. Below is a brief outline of the method used to estimate the additional costs. (A more detailed explanation of my assumptions and procedures appears in the appendix.)

For many years after 1952 the Military Sealift Command procured space aboard U.S. flag liners at rates that apparently reflected vessel operating costs before payment of the operating differential subsidy. The rates were remunerative not only to subsidized lines but also to unsubsidized lines. If the command instead had purchased space from foreign flag liners, it no doubt would have paid considerably lower rates, reflecting the lower costs of foreign flag operation. During much of this period the operating costs of foreign carriers were roughly half those of U.S. carriers. Accordingly I estimate that the command's shipping costs for liner space might well have been halved.

26. AIMS, Maritime Subsidy Board Docket S-244, exhibit 56.
27. The command also paid many hundreds of millions of dollars to commercial interests for the operation of most of the tankers in the MSC nucleus fleet and of government-owned vessels from the National Defense Reserve Fleet; but these sums are ignored throughout the discussion.

In 1966 the Defense Department adopted a new method of procuring liner space, one that resembled competitive bidding. If the department's demand for shipping space had not been increasing rapidly, shipping rates should have fallen toward the level of U.S. vessel operating costs *after* subsidy. This would have greatly narrowed the difference between the freight rates the command paid and those it would have paid to foreign carriers. But owing to the command's growing demand for shipping space during the military buildup in Vietnam, shipping rates apparently remained at a level just sufficient to cover costs *before* subsidy payments. And so I estimate that between 1966 and 1969 the MSC must have paid shipping rates that were nearly twice as high as it would have paid to foreign lines.

After 1969 the demand for space diminished, shipping rates apparently fell relative to operating costs, and the difference between U.S. and foreign rates must have narrowed. I estimate that the command paid between 15 percent and one-third more for shipping space than foreign lines would have charged.

Since the Maritime Administration pays no operating subsidy for sailings under charter, the charter rates for American ships must have reflected their higher operating expenses, and since the operators received no subsidy, the operating expenses were the actual costs that the operators paid. With foreign costs approximately half of American costs, U.S. flag vessels must have charged roughly twice the charter rates of similar foreign flag vessels—a conclusion supported by personnel in the Department of Agriculture who monitor U.S. and foreign charter rates and who have used this ratio as their rule of thumb for years.

Using financial data from the records of the Military Sealift Command, I estimate that the exclusive use of U.S. vessels must have added approximately $3.8 billion to military shipping costs between 1952 and 1972—a larger sum than the government spent for the operating differential subsidy during the same period. Table 7-4 breaks this figure down into annual totals. Although this estimate of nearly $4 billion is by no means a precise one—the true cost may have been as little as $3 billion, or as much as $5 billion—it is more likely to err on the low side than on the high. But whether it does or not, the principal conclusion to be drawn is that the costs of the cargo preference laws have been considerable—certainly much greater than others have hitherto assumed.

Table 7-4. Commercial Payments by Military Sealift Command for Space Aboard Liners and Charter of Vessels, and Imputed Cargo Preference Laws Subsidy, Fiscal Years 1952–72

Millions of dollars

Fiscal year	Commercial payments			Imputed subsidy due to cargo preference laws
	For space aboard liners	*For charter of vessels*	*Total*	
1952	147.4	250.0	397.4	198.7
1953	172.8	253.8	426.6	213.3
1954	146.5	163.9	310.3	155.2
1955	142.5	66.2	208.7	104.3
1956	150.9	58.7	209.6	104.8
1957	177.6	37.4	215.0	107.5
1958	174.9	43.0	217.8	108.9
1959	179.6	63.1	242.6	121.3
1960	163.0	54.5	217.5	108.7
1961	153.0	61.8	214.8	107.4
1962	189.2	84.3	273.6	136.8
1963	203.2	82.7	285.9	143.0
1964	204.9	88.9	293.8	146.9
1965	202.1	90.1	292.2	146.1
1966	261.8	255.9	517.7	258.9
1967	300.9	371.6	672.5	294.1
1968	317.7	479.3	797.0	341.3
1969	366.1	480.3	846.4	342.7
1970	343.9	435.2	779.1	279.5
1971	306.9	340.9	647.9	201.2
1972	305.4	315.0	620.4	175.8
Total	4,610.2	4,076.4	8,686.7	3,796.3

Source: Same as Table 7-3. Figures are rounded and may not add to totals.

Food for Peace Cargoes

Food for Peace is the popular name for the activities carried out under the Agricultural Trade Development and Assistance Act of 1954.[28] It is primarily a program for financing the sale of agricultural commodities on liberal credit terms to less developed countries. Most of the food that moves abroad is bought by the recipient nations at roughly the same

28. Act of July 10, 1954, 68 Stat. 454. This act is also known as P.L. 480— Public Law 480 of the Eighty-third Congress—and the cargoes it gives rise to are called P.L. 480 cargoes.

prices as those prevailing in world markets. But the terms of payment are far more generous than those usually available from private dealers: the Commodity Credit Corporation (an agency of the Department of Agriculture) typically finances the full amount of the sale; no down payment is asked of the purchasing country; and repayment usually begins after a number of years. Low rates of interest are charged on these loans, often no more than 2 percent or 3 percent a year. In some cases countries may take as long as forty years to repay. Between 1955 and 1974, no country has defaulted.

In view of these liberal provisions, the sales program is clearly akin to foreign assistance—even in the name "long-term concessional sales" by which these transactions are known.[29]

Public Law 480 also authorizes gifts of food—called donations—from the United States to less developed countries. There are two such donative programs: one popularly called the government-to-government program, the other the voluntary agencies program. Under the first, the President may furnish food from government stocks to foreign nations to meet emergency needs, promote economic development, relieve malnutrition, or for other similar purposes. Under the second, he may furnish commodities to voluntary relief agencies and international organizations that will superintend their distribution in less developed countries in pursuit of the same aims.

In addition to authorizing sales and donations, P.L. 480 also established a barter program. A sizable movement of goods took place from 1954 to 1963, as the government bartered agricultural commodities abroad for materials to be added to the nation's strategic stockpiles. After 1963 the use of P.L. 480 barters dwindled, and in 1968 the program ended. Although the government is still bartering agricultural commodities—no longer to build up strategic stockpiles, but to acquire the goods and services that government agencies need overseas—it is doing so under the authority of the Commodity Credit Corporation Charter Act instead of P.L. 480.

29. At one time the concessional element took a quite different form. Countries were obliged to pay for their purchases soon after receiving the commodities—but with payment accepted in the country's own currency, rather than in one of the world's hard currencies. Beginning in 1961 an increasing proportion of sales have been made on credit, with terms that provide for payment in dollars or a convertible local currency. In 1966 Congress directed that after December 31, 1971, no sales should be made for nonconvertible currencies. Henceforth all sales must be credit sales and must be paid for in dollars.

Of the three Food for Peace programs—sales, donations, and barters —the sales program has been the largest. Between 1954 and 1972 nearly 71 percent by value of all P.L. 480 exports were commodities that had been sold to foreign nations, over 20 percent were donations, and 8 percent barters.[30] Sales have decreased since 1964, barters ceased in 1968, while donations have stayed about the same; so donations now constitute about 30 percent of Food for Peace shipments.[31]

P.L. 480 shipments have accounted for a sizable fraction of all cargoes carried by U.S. flag vessels since deliveries began in 1954. Statistics for the sales program show that from 1955 through 1970 15.3 percent by weight of all cargoes carried by U.S. flag vessels in U.S. foreign commerce were agricultural exports being delivered to foreign nations under Food for Peace sales agreements.[32] In the peak years of 1963 and 1964 this fraction rose to just over one-quarter. If similar figures were available for the movement of donated commodities, they no doubt would show that U.S. flag vessels depended on Food for Peace programs for at least one-fifth of the cargoes they carried in U.S. foreign commerce from 1955 through 1970.

Most P.L. 480 cargoes fall within the compass of the 1954 Cargo Preference Act. At least half of them must therefore be carried in privately owned U.S. flag vessels. Nevertheless, between July 1, 1954, and June 30, 1972, only 48.7 percent of the commodities sold under P.L. 480 sales agreements were shipped overseas in U.S. vessels. The balance moved in foreign vessels. In thirteen of the eighteen fiscal years from 1955 through 1972, U.S. flag vessels did carry more than half of all shipments, but in four of the other five years their share fell well under half: in 1957 owing to a shortage of shipping when the Suez Canal was closed, and later in the 1960s owing to the demand of the armed services for transport to Vietnam.

ADDED COST TO SALES PROGRAM. The costs to the nation of the cargo preference laws are in no case more accurately known than in connection

30. *Annual Report on Activities Carried Out under Public Law 480, 83rd Congress, as Amended, during the Period January 1 through December 31, 1972,* table 1, p. 73.

31. Donations were abnormally high in 1972, when emergency aid was sent to Bangladesh. Since 1972 the quantity of goods moving abroad each year under all P.L. 480 programs has fallen sharply; but the *value* of shipments has declined only moderately. By either measure sales have declined more than donations.

32. Statistics of P.L. 480 shipments aboard U.S. flag vessels were supplied by the Department of Agriculture, Export Marketing Service, Ocean Transportation Division. Statistics of all shipments aboard U.S. flag vessels were taken from *Annual Report of the Maritime Administration for Fiscal Year 1971,* p. 75.

with the P.L. 480 sales program. The reason for this is that, besides financing the sale of commodities, the Commodity Credit Corporation may also finance a part of the cost of shipping them to their foreign destinations when U.S. vessels are employed as the carriers. The part it may pay is the excess of the cost of shipment in the U.S. vessel over the cost of shipment in a foreign vessel, a difference known as the "ocean freight differential." The buyer is not obliged to repay this sum, as it must repay the loan it received to purchase the commodity. It is therefore the corporation—and ultimately the U.S. taxpayer—that pays the additional cost of transporting the commodity in U.S. vessels.

In no instance can an ocean freight differential be measured directly. No item appears under this heading on any invoice for shipping services. Freight differentials can only be estimated by specialists who keep abreast of world shipping prices. When a U.S. shipping company presents its bill to the importing country, the country applies to the Commodity Credit Corporation for reimbursement in the amount of the differential. The corporation has already estimated what the cost would have been to have shipped the commodity in a foreign vessel. It subtracts this sum from the freight actually paid and remits the difference to the buyer.

Because the ocean freight differential is an actual charge against the corporation, and no mere bookkeeping entry, an accurate record has been kept of its cost. By June 30, 1971, the cost had reached $840.1 million since the sales program began in 1955.[33] Annual freight differential payments were largest during the mid-sixties. As shipments under the sales program have declined recently, annual expenditures have also fallen, from a high of $81.1 million in fiscal 1967 to $50.1 million in 1971.

Before its authority to do so was withdrawn by Congress in 1966, the Commodity Credit Corporation often financed the *full* costs of shipment aboard U.S. flag vessels, not just the ocean freight differential. When commodities were sold for foreign currencies the U.S. carrier that delivered the goods applied directly to the corporation for payment of the freight. The corporation paid the carrier in U.S. dollars, and the foreign buyer paid the U.S. government the equivalent in its own currency of the cost of shipment in a foreign flag vessel. This amount was called the "foreign flag equivalent cost." The balance was the ocean freight differential, which then as now was absorbed by the corporation. As a result of these and

33. U.S. Department of Agriculture, Commodity Credit Corporation, *Report of Financial Condition and Operations as of June 30, 1971,* schedules 18 and 19, pp. 34–35.

other transactions, the United States accumulated large holdings of several nonconvertible currencies—larger in fact than it could efficiently use. In these cases the payments that the U.S. government received from foreign buyers were practically worthless, and U.S. taxpayers, through the Commodity Credit Corporation, ended up paying nearly the full costs of shipping the commodities in U.S. flag vessels.

The question arises whether these foreign flag equivalent costs should be added to the ocean freight differential payments to determine the total costs of cargo preference. Lawrence thought so and included $48.8 million as an estimate of these additional costs for 1962.[34] Although a plausible case can be made for including them, they have not been included in these estimates on the grounds that they are more properly treated as a form of foreign assistance than as a cost of cargo preference.[35] Whoever disagrees may add to the costs of cargo preference all or a part of the $516.4 million representing costs of shipment aboard foreign flag vessels that U.S. authorities paid to U.S. carriers between the fiscal years

34. Lawrence, *U.S. Merchant Shipping*, p. 364.

35. The point is certainly debatable. I reasoned as follows. Once the United States had decided to establish a foreign assistance program, it might have felt obliged to pay at least a part of the costs of transporting P.L. 480 commodities to foreign buyers, even if no cargo preference laws existed. Suppose the United States had considered selling the commodities free on board at an American port, leaving it to the buyers to arrange their own transportation. Foreign countries would then have had to expend scarce hard currency to hire the vessels of other nations to transport the cargoes, assuming that their own fleets were not large enough to do the job themselves. If it was U.S. policy to help developing countries maintain their hard currency reserves, the United States might have had to expand other aid programs to offset the recipients' currency expenditures for ocean transportation. In that case the United States would one way or another have borne some of the costs of shipping the commodities, regardless of the preference laws.

It is important to assume that the merchant fleets of the countries that bought P.L. 480 commodities had no extra capacity to carry more of the commodities than they already were doing. Although this assumption is difficult to verify, I believe it is justified. Between 1954 and 1966 the principal buyers of agricultural commodities that the United States sold for foreign currencies were (by size of purchase, in decreasing order) India, Pakistan, Egypt, Yugoslavia, Poland, Brazil, Republic of Korea, Turkey, and Spain. More than three-quarters of all sales were made to these countries. (*Annual Report of the President on Activities Carried Out under Public Law 480, 83rd Congress, as Amended, during the Period January 1 through December 31, 1966*, table 2, pp. 58–61.) Only India and Spain possessed as much as 1 percent of the world's commercial tonnage on December 31, 1966 (1.2 percent and 1.1 percent respectively, by gross registered tonnage). (U.S. Maritime Administration, *Merchant Fleets of the World: Oceangoing Steam and Motor Ships of 1,000 Gross Tons and Over as of December 31, 1966*.) Much of the Indian fleet had been acquired only lately.

1955 and 1967.[36] My preference would be to add the entire amount—
if anything is to be added at all—although Lawrence included only about
three-quarters of the payments that were made in fiscal 1963.[37]

ADDED COST TO DONATIONS. Like commodities shipped under P.L. 480
sales agreements, donated commodities are also subject to the provisions
of the 1954 Cargo Preference Act. A question has been raised whether
this act is strictly applicable to shipments under the voluntary agencies
program; but the Agency for International Development, which administers both the voluntary agencies and government-to-government programs, has never contested the common view that it is and has regularly
urged the agencies that are responsible for arranging transport of the
commodities to use U.S. flag vessels whenever possible.[38] As a result of
AID's persuasion, the fraction of donative shipments that U.S. flag vessels
have carried has generally been well in excess of the minimum of 50 percent that the law requires.

Only the roughest estimate can be offered of how much the cargo preference laws have added to the cost of shipping donated commodities
abroad. The U.S. government pays the full cost of moving them to their
foreign destinations, whether shipment is made aboard U.S. flag or foreign
flag vessels. The Agency for International Development is therefore under

36. Commodity Credit Corporation, *Report of Financial Condition and Operations as of June 30, 1971,* schedule 18, p. 34. This figure is obtained as the difference
between total ocean transportation payments and payments of ocean freight
differential.

37. According to the U.S. Agricultural Stabilization and Conservation Service,
total U.S. payments of foreign flag equivalent costs were $67.5 million in fiscal 1963.
Lawrence apparently included only payments to U.S. carriers for which the United
States received reimbursement in currencies "which had officially been declared
excess to U.S. needs" (Lawrence, *U.S. Merchant Shipping,* p. 364, note b). It is
questionable, however, whether a distinction is warranted between currencies that
had been officially declared excess to U.S. needs and others that had not. Nearly
all the currencies in which the United States was reimbursed were nonconvertible
currencies, of which this country already had a surplus. Whether they had been
declared excess currencies or not is really of no moment. In all cases the incremental
value of additions to U.S. holdings must have been zero, or nearly zero.

38. The Agency for International Development administers most current foreign aid programs (reviewed in the following section) as well as these donations.
AID was established in 1961 to consolidate the functions of the International Cooperation Administration and the Development Loan Fund, as well as to perform
whatever additional duties were assigned to it by the Foreign Assistance Act of 1961
and subsequent legislation. For brevity's sake, the name AID is used to refer to all
of these agencies, including those that were replaced by the Agency for International
Development in 1961. For data on AID programs, see AID, Office of Statistics and
Reports, *Operations Report,* published annually.

no obligation to compute an ocean freight differential whenever foreign carriers are used, as the Ocean Transportation Division in the Department of Agriculture must do in connection with shipments of sold commodities. As a result, the cost of the cargo preference laws has to be calculated from the few aggregate figures that AID does record.

Almost all donative commodities shipped by the voluntary agencies move abroad in small lots aboard cargo liners, in contrast to commodities moving under the P.L. 480 sales program, most of which are carried in shipload lots aboard tramp steamers. Nothing in the scanty records that AID maintains indicates whether foreign flag liners would have carried these goods more cheaply than U.S. flag liners. AID personnel say that the great majority of the goods shipped by voluntary agencies aboard U.S. flag liners move at conference rates, and that therefore no savings would be realized if the commodities were carried by foreign flag vessels. For the reasons given above this conclusion does not follow. Even if all such shipments traveled at conference rates, the cargo preference laws must have maintained these rates at a higher level than they would otherwise have been. How much higher no one can say. During fiscal 1955–72 the U.S. government spent $610 million for ocean transportation under this program. How much less would it have spent if the cargo preference laws had not been in force? Fifty million dollars is probably a conservative figure.

Official records of the commodities shipped under the government-to-government program are also sparse. It is only possible to say that most traveled aboard cargo liners and the rest aboard tramps, and that between fiscal 1961 and fiscal 1972 just over 80 percent of all freight payments for government-to-government shipments were received by U.S. carriers. If U.S. carriers also received about 80 percent of the payments before 1961, they have been paid about $340 million since the program began.[39] Suppose that of this sum tramp operators received about $100 million and

39. Between July 1, 1956, and June 30, 1972, the U.S. government paid $426 million to carriers of all nations to transport farm commodities to foreign destinations under the P.L. 480 government-to-government program. The program had been established on July 10, 1954, when P.L. 480 became law, but it was not until enactment of the Agricultural Act of 1956 that the federal government was authorized not only to furnish the commodities without any charge but to pay the costs of their shipment to overseas ports. Evidently the costs had previously been borne by the recipient nations. All freight payments cited in this section are payments by the U.S. government, not by foreign nations, since the purpose here is to determine the cost of the preference laws to U.S. taxpayers, not their cost to others.

liner operators the rest. Suppose next that the costs of shipment aboard U.S. tramps were roughly twice as great as the costs aboard foreign flag tramps, as records of the Department of Agriculture suggest. Then the difference of $50 million measures the costs of compliance with the cargo preference laws.

Now consider shipments aboard U.S. cargo liners. Since most of these commodities were conference-rated, there is no direct way of telling how much lower shipping costs would have been in the absence of the cargo preference laws. A conservative guess would be that shipping costs would have been lowered by at least $25 million since 1956.

In sum, the cargo preference requirements of federal law may have added more than $125 million to the costs of shipping farm commodities that the U.S. government has donated to foreign nations since 1954 under the voluntary agencies and government-to-government programs of P.L. 480.[40]

Foreign Aid Cargoes

Another important class of preference cargoes consists of goods moving abroad under the U.S. civilian foreign aid programs, exclusive of the Food for Peace program. Most current aid programs are administered by the Agency for International Development. AID ships no foreign aid cargoes itself. Instead it makes loans and grants to foreign countries, which in turn use these funds to purchase goods for delivery abroad. Commodities whose purchase is financed by AID must be shipped in conformity with the requirements of the Cargo Preference Act of 1954. Therefore, a minimum of one-half of all shipments must be carried in privately owned U.S. flag vessels. Similar preference requirements were contained in earlier foreign assistance legislation. Since 1948 the great majority of all aid shipments, with the exception of those aboard tankers, have moved

40. U.S. contributions to the World Food Program (a joint undertaking of the United Nations and the Food and Agriculture Organization) are usually distinguished from the donations made under the Food for Peace programs, despite the fact that U.S. participation in the World Food Program is authorized in the same title of P.L. 480 that authorizes the other programs. Most of the U.S. contributions are in the form of farm commodities, with the United States also paying the cost of their delivery to foreign nations. These cargo movements are subject to the Cargo Preference Act of 1954, and it is fair to conclude that the costs of shipment have therefore been increased. These movements have not been taken into account in the cost estimates here, primarily because they have been considerably smaller than the movements generated by the voluntary agencies and government-to-government programs.

in U.S. flag vessels. No statistics are available by tonnage; but of shipping payments amounting to $2,658 million between fiscal 1948 and fiscal 1970 for the transport of AID-financed commodities, $2,075 million, or 78 percent, were paid to U.S. flag carriers.[41] Just over 80 percent of all payments to liner and tramp operators were made to U.S. flag operators, but only 54 percent of payments to tanker operators. For the last several years, however, the fractions have been nearly 100 percent in all three classes, as shippers of AID-financed cargoes have employed U.S. flag vessels almost exclusively.

Between 1948 and 1970 AID paid U.S. tramp operators $645 million for the transport of aid cargoes overseas, and U.S. tanker operators $180 million: a total of $825 million. Assuming that throughout this period shippers could have engaged foreign flag vessels to carry shipload lots of aid cargo at roughly half the price received by U.S. flag operators, approximately $400 million in shipping costs might have been saved. Of the cargoes that moved aboard U.S. flag liners, AID is only able to state that the great majority moved at conference rates rather than at open rates. Suppose that 20 percent of the $1,296 million of freight payments for AID-financed cargoes on U.S. flag liners was paid for the shipment of open-rated commodities, say $250 million. If foreign flag vessels were willing to accept the same cargoes at half the shipping rate, somewhat more than $100 million of shipping costs might have been saved. Another $100 million might have been saved on the shipment of conference-rated commodities if they had not been reserved for U.S. flag vessels. Adding these sums to the $400 million obtained from the statistics for tramps and tankers yields the round figure of $600 million as a rough measure of the extra cost of using U.S. flag vessels to transport foreign aid cargoes between 1948 and 1970.

Miscellaneous Programs

There are several other government programs that generate a regular flow of preference cargo. The agencies in charge of these programs maintain no shipping statistics worth mentioning; but their cargoes clearly are meager beside shipments of military supplies, Food for Peace commodities, and foreign aid cargoes. Accordingly there is no point in preparing

41. Unpublished figures supplied by the Agency for International Development, Resources Transportation Division.

what would necessarily be quite arbitrary estimates of the costs that the cargo preference laws add to their operation.

To take one example, the largest remaining movement of preference cargo is apparently the transport of U.S. products to foreign buyers in cases where the Export-Import Bank of the United States has financed the purchase. All such shipments are subject to the requirements of Public Resolution 17, one of the cargo preference provisions discussed above. According to statistics published during the "double subsidy" hearing before the Maritime Subsidy Board, just over 1 million long tons of bank-financed exports were transported in U.S. flag vessels from 1964 to 1969 inclusive.[42] All of these shipments moved on liners. By comparison, outbound military shipments aboard U.S. flag vessels during the same six years totaled nearly 33 million long tons. Even so small a program as the donative Food for Peace program that is administered through registered voluntary agencies accounted for the movement of considerably more cargo throughout this period than bank-financed exports.

It is tempting to say of bank-financed exports that even when shipping costs are increased by the preference laws, the increment is borne by the foreign buyer, not by the U.S. taxpayer, who pays the cost of cargo preference in other programs. This would only be true, however, if the demand for U.S. exports were unaffected by small increases in price. If the more reasonable assumption is made that the extra cost of "shipping American" will occasionally cause a customer to decide against buying the American product—or against buying as much of the product—the cost will be borne not wholly by the buyer but by the U.S. producer also. Or the U.S. supplier may shade his price and voluntarily absorb a portion of the freight differential to remain competitive with foreign suppliers, in which case the same result is reached directly.

42. AIMS, Maritime Subsidy Board Docket S-244, exhibit 33.

CHAPTER EIGHT

Economic Objectives
of Maritime Assistance

THE GOVERNMENT grants public aid to the maritime industries in order to accomplish certain political, economic, and military objectives. This chapter examines the economic rationale that supporters have used to justify this aid. The principal economic benefits they cite are the favorable effects of a prosperous U.S. merchant marine on the balance of payments, employment, and public revenues. But the economic arguments have seldom been presented with the care they deserve; supporters of maritime assistance seldom explain why assistance is warranted and what national objectives it serves. They often substitute bombast for reason and flag-waving for solid analysis. Some supporters of course are more thoughtful. Several years ago an industry group commissioned a study to measure the foreign exchange savings that may be credited to the operations of the American merchant marine.[1] Even this careful review, however, makes no attempt to evaluate the balance of payments argument that the value of these savings is one good reason for subsidizing the U.S. maritime industries. Other reports have occasionally paid lip service to the objectives of the maritime program but included little useful analysis.[2] A very few studies have called attention to these omissions and recommended that the objec-

1. Harbridge House, "The Balance of Payments and the U.S. Merchant Marine" (Boston: Harbridge House, Inc., 1968; processed); reprinted in James R. Barker and Robert Brandwein, *The United States Merchant Marine in National Perspective* (Heath Lexington Books, 1970), app. C.
2. The latest example, by a presidential commission appointed in 1971, is the *Report of the Commission on American Shipbuilding*, three volumes (Washington, D.C.: the Commission, 1973). Although the report includes much valuable material, the commission was perfunctory in stating why assistance to the maritime industries is warranted. In the commission's defense, its terms of reference did not authorize it to reexamine the bases for the program.

tives of the assistance program should be spelled out concretely.[3] The authors of one such study actually did state how large a merchant marine was needed to satisfy national defense needs (discussed in chapter 9) and based their recommendations on that number. But the supporting details were said to be classified and were not presented.[4]

Employment and Output Effects

The principal economic argument for assisting the U.S. maritime industries is the balance of payments argument reviewed in the following section. But some supporters of the maritime program have also emphasized the favorable employment effects of the program, its addition to gross national product, and the extra tax revenues that the program generates.[5] Apparently no one has ever suggested that these effects constitute a sufficient reason for continuing the program, as if it were a public works project as valuable for the employment it gives as for its tangible product. But since they are apt to be included in any accounting of the program's costs and benefits—diminishing the former or adding to the latter—their validity ought to be considered. To the extent that the effects are genuine, fewer other benefits would need to be demonstrated for the program to justify its cost.

There are immediate difficulties. How the data are derived that measure the economic effects of the program has never been carefully explained. It appears that they are computed in a very simple manner. To take one example, it was reported that "2.1 million man-years of employment

3. See, for example, Arthur D. Little, Inc., "Ship Construction Differential Subsidies," Report to the Maritime Administration, U.S. Department of Commerce (1961; processed):

"The fundamental problem of the construction subsidy program is . . . the absence of specific defense objectives for the subsidized shipbuilding industry. . . . It is strongly recommended that the national defense need for shipbuilding capabilities be examined in detail, and that these needs [sic] be expressed in terms of the specific amounts of construction capacity and labor skills that must be maintained by subsidy in order to provide the necessary defense posture in shipbuilding" (pp. 16, 19).

4. U.S. Interagency Maritime Task Force, "The Merchant Marine in National Defense and Trade: A Policy and a Program" (1965; processed), p. 5, note 1.

5. See, for example, the *Report of the Commission on American Shipbuilding,* and Joseph Kasputys and Joe Bill Young, "Subsidies, Seed Money, and National Security," *Seapower,* vol. 16 (September 1973), pp. 23–30 (the authors were the director of the Office of Policy and Plans of the Maritime Administration and an economist with the Maritime Administration respectively).

would be generated to build and operate the vessels [needed to carry all U.S. oceanborne imports of oil and gas in 1985]," and that "a $57 billion expansion in gross national product (GNP) would be generated [by the same program]."[6] The authors do not explain how they obtained these numbers, but apparently the employment figures are just the sum of the man-years required to build and operate the ships. That is, the employment totals apparently are *gross* totals, not *net* totals, meaning that no allowance has been made for the reduction in employment that occurs elsewhere in the economy when resources are diverted to the shipbuilding and ship operating industries. The steel used in a ship might otherwise be used in the framework of a new building. The welders that work on a ship's hull might find employment on construction projects elsewhere. The engineer who tends a ship's machinery might otherwise become a building engineer. In short, if the resources—both human and material—that are devoted to the maritime program could find employment elsewhere in the event that the program ceased, it is wrong to say that the program has generated employment or added to the nation's economic product.

Effect on the Economy

Some of these analysts go further and include among the program's effects on employment and production its derivative effects throughout the economy—the multiplier effects that are discussed so often in connection with public employment programs. The basic idea is both simple and sound. A part of every dollar of wages is spent by the recipient, and at least a part of this expenditure is a wage to someone else. This second recipient in turn spends part of his receipt and so pays part of the wage of a third person. The chain continues through a large number of recipients. In this manner the initial payment of one dollar in wages ultimately generates much more than a dollar of wage payments throughout the economy. Expenditures for materials are treated in the same way. And so the construction of a ship that costs $50 million to build might generate, say, a total of $150 million of economic activity throughout the economy if the multiplier is three.

The same stipulation concerning the resources directly employed in the program holds true here. Only if the resources that are purchased on the second, third, and succeeding rounds of the expenditure chain would

6. Kasputys and Young, "Subsidies, Seed Money, and National Security," p. 23.

otherwise be unemployed is it correct to include them in a tally of the employment effects of the program. If only some of the resources would be newly employed, their employment alone should be counted. The effective multiplier would thus not be three but some number less than three, say, for example, one and a half. Accordingly the additional economic activity generated by the construction of a ship costing $50 million might not be $150 million but, say, one-tenth as much, just $15 million, if only one-fifth of the cost of building the ship—$10 million—consisted of payments for resources that would otherwise have lain idle, and if the proper multiplier to use were not three but one and a half.

It should thus be clear that in order to evaluate the economic effects of the maritime program one has to identify the alternative employment opportunities of the resources it uses. Only to the extent that the program uses resources that would otherwise be idle may it be said to add to economic activity. This point is seldom made explicit in published descriptions of the maritime program. Admittedly it is not easy to decide what fraction of employment is new employment. Consider the labor used to build a new ship. Even if all of the workers had come from other jobs to work on the ship, their old jobs might have been filled in part by men who were previously unemployed. In that case the building of the ship generated no new employment directly, but did generate employment at one or two stages removed.

Is it impossible then to venture any conclusions concerning the employment effects of the current maritime program? No, not if it is understood that the conclusions must be tentative, based on very slender evidence. Kasputys and Young said in their 1973 report that "the jobs involved [in a major shipbuilding program] would employ people that would not otherwise be employed."[7] They cite no authority for their statement, and in fact it seems to be contradicted by evidence elsewhere. The recent report of the Commission on American Shipbuilding included remarks about the difficulty shipbuilders have experienced in hiring and retaining skilled employees:

> The [shipbuilding] industry experiences difficulty in obtaining skilled workers even though the Shipbuilders Council and the Maritime Administration estimated the level of work force employed in 1972 was only 60 to 65 percent of the optimal employment that could have been absorbed by the existing facilities. . . .
> The shortage of skilled manpower has been apparent for at least the past

7. Ibid., p. 25.

four years in the major shipyards. Most of the yards have continuously advertised for skilled personnel. Practically all of the larger shipyards have apprentice schools in operation. While this is one answer to the problem, it has only met with marginal success. In many instances after employees are trained, they have been enticed to the higher paying jobs in the construction industry. The critical craft shortages include pipefitters, welders, shipfitters, machinists and electricians. . . .

Shipyards find that when they attempt to recall employees after a layoff, the most productive and highly trained workers have taken jobs elsewhere and are lost to their former employers.[8]

Apparently these references are to skilled workers only, not to workers at all skill levels. Perhaps other classes of employees can be recruited from among unemployed persons. But if these observations are reliable, they suggest that the great majority of persons employed in the building of ships would not remain without jobs for long if the shipbuilding program were reduced or terminated.

Effect on Public Revenues

Supporters of the maritime program sometimes argue that assistance to these industries is really costless, because the resulting expansion of economic activity increases tax revenues by more than the sums that are given to the industries. The preceding discussion answers this argument also. Unless the shipbuilding program produces a *net* expansion of employment and output, it can hardly lead to other than trivial increases in aggregate public revenue.

But the argument is open to another—and basic—objection. The government is not a profit-making enterprise whose operations should be evaluated on the basis of a profit and loss statement. It is sensible to ask what are the employment and output effects of a particular government program, or equivalently, what use does the program make of resources that would otherwise be idle. It is not very sensible, on the other hand, to calculate the government's share of the net increase in economic output and then judge how valuable the program is by whether that share is at least as great as the program's direct public cost. Although this procedure resembles a benefit-cost calculation, it is fundamentally quite different. The full costs of the maritime program are not measured by its cost to the

8. *Report of the Commission on American Shipbuilding*, vol. 2, pp. 24, 25. The second paragraph is from a statement made in 1970 by the maritime administrator.

Treasury, which after all is no "cost" at all but—in the case of subsidies—
a transfer. The real costs of the program are its resource costs—the materials and labor that the program consumes. Even more important, the
benefits of the program bear no relation whatsoever to the additional taxes,
if any, that the Treasury collects from an expansion in output. The
Treasury's receipts and disbursements merely measure certain financial
transfers that are incidental to the program and tell nothing of its cost
or value to the community.

It might be objected that a comparison of receipts and disbursements
at least indicates how the program affects the size of the public sector,
hence what costs it imposes on other public programs, assuming that the
community takes no steps to modify these effects. But this assumption is
patently artificial. Maritime program or no maritime program, the community has the power to devote whatever fraction it wishes of its economic
product to activities financed through the public sector. The maritime
program need take nothing from other public activities even without any
expansion in the nation's economic output if tax rates are properly
adjusted.

In view of the above disabilities, it would be better if the net effect of
the maritime program on public revenues were not reviewed and analyzed
since such discussion is apt to be more confusing and misleading than
enlightening.

Effect on Balance of Payments

The chief economic rationale for public aid to the maritime industries
is the balance of payments argument. Supporters of maritime assistance
allege that the American merchant marine (the shipbuilding industry is
discussed later) contributes greatly to a positive U.S. balance of payments
by earning and conserving an unusually large amount of foreign exchange
per dollar of output. The industry *earns* foreign exchange by selling a
large part of its product to foreigners. But the sale of the rest of its product
to residents of the United States also improves the U.S. balance of payments, because it saves—or *conserves*—for this country the foreign exchange that would otherwise be spent to buy the same services from foreign operators. The entire output of the industry is thus said to be either
foreign exchange earning or foreign exchange saving, in contrast to the
output of other industries, of which normally only a part is foreign ex-

change earning or saving. According to its supporters, the industry's unique efficiency as earner and conserver of foreign exchange abundantly justifies public assistance.

Such is the argument in brief. It contains much truth, but not the whole truth, focusing as it does exclusively on outputs. The shipping industry's *net* effect on the U.S. balance of payments—and it is the industry's net effect that is of interest—cannot be measured without examining the industry's inputs. The U.S. merchant marine is a major consumer of foreign goods and services. Like ship operators everywhere, U.S. operators ordinarily purchase fuel, stores, or labor services wherever their vessels call. In foreign ports, for example, ships must be loaded and unloaded by foreign longshoremen, who are paid in local currency. These purchases greatly subtract from the industry's foreign exchange earnings. As a result U.S. ships by no means earn or conserve as much foreign exchange as the industry's output figures alone would indicate.[9]

For the same reasons, American patronage of foreign vessels is not nearly as costly in foreign exchange as might at first be supposed. Just as domestic operators must buy some goods and services abroad, foreign carriers serving American ports must make large purchases of goods and services in the United States. Therefore only a portion of the payments that local shippers make to foreign operators is a net expenditure of foreign exchange.[10]

Accordingly it is incorrect to say that every dollar—or its equivalent in foreign currency—that is paid to the American fleet for transportation services is a dollar's worth of foreign exchange earned or saved.[11] This

---

9. If U.S. operators also purchased their ships abroad, as many operators elsewhere do, the industry's net foreign exchange earnings would be even smaller. But nearly all ships for the U.S. merchant marine are built in this country.

10. These points have of course been made before. See, for example, "Investment in Shipping and the Balance of Payments: A Case-Study of Import-Substitution Policy," chap. 3 in R. O. Goss, *Studies in Maritime Economics* (Cambridge: Cambridge University Press, 1968), and the references cited there.

11. This is a good point at which to observe that the conventional balance of payments argument, as recited above, contains several additional assumptions that are sometimes made explicit, but often are not. For example, one is expected to assume that in the absence of a U.S. fleet the nation's commerce would be carried by foreign ships at unchanged freight rates. To the extent that freight rates would rise, the foreign exchange savings attributable to the U.S. fleet are even greater than supposed. Or the savings may be less, if foreign ships would charge less. There is no reason to review these assumptions here since most of them are plausible, or at least not less plausible than the alternatives.

is now widely recognized, though not always remembered. How much of each dollar really represents net earnings or savings of foreign exchange? One 1966 study prepared within the Maritime Administration concluded that of every dollar paid to the U.S. merchant marine the average net gain to the U.S. balance of payments is just 30 cents.[12] This figure was challenged in a later study, in which it was claimed that the true figure is either 42 cents or 50 cents, depending on whether it is commercial cargo or defense cargo that the ships are carrying.[13] The study was commissioned by an association of U.S. steamship lines and its authors were obviously at pains to show that the shipping industry had greatly improved the U.S. balance of payments. But aside from one important error in it, the study appears to have been done with care. Its figures for the years 1957 through 1966 are still among the best estimates available of the balance of payments impact of the U.S. merchant marine. These disclose that for the years 1957 through 1966, the positive effect on the U.S. balance of payments of all U.S. merchant shipping operations totaled $7.3 billion.[14] This estimate is certainly too high. The authors apparently assumed that the Department of Defense would have paid foreign carriers the same freight rates for transportation services that it actually paid U.S. carriers if the former instead of the latter had carried defense cargoes. Foreign carriage would surely have been cheaper; hence foreign exchange savings were less than they thought. Rough estimates suggest that the true figure for the ten years may lie between $5 billion and $6 billion.

Even an estimate of $5 billion or $6 billion exaggerates the net impact of U.S. merchant shipping operations on the nation's balance of payments. In preparing this estimate the authors did not take into account how the resources employed in shipping might otherwise have been used and what their effect would have been on the balance of payments. If the fleet had terminated operations in the 1960s there would have been some balance of payments gains to offset the loss of the fleet's earnings. The sale of U.S. flag vessels to foreign buyers would have had a sizable, if temporary, positive impact on the U.S. balance of payments. There would have been a continuing gain as some maritime labor moved into industries that export a part of their product (which could then expand production and sales abroad), or into industries whose products substitute for imports. Obvi-

12. Reported in Harbridge House, "The Balance of Payments and the U.S. Merchant Marine," pp. 22–23.
   13. Ibid., p. 35.
   14. Ibid., p. 7.

ously the size of the balance of payments gain would depend on circumstances that are difficult to foretell. What industries would absorb the maritime labor force? How much would these industries increase production? What part of the increase would be exported? Precise answers are impossible, but it must be expected that ultimately there would be some improvement in the balance of payments as the displaced labor found employment elsewhere in the economy. It is unlikely that the gain would offset more than a small or moderate fraction of the loss of the fleet's export earnings, but still it cannot be ignored.[15]

Suppose we say that the impact of the U.S. merchant fleet on the U.S. balance of payments between 1957 and 1966 was $5 billion, even though it probably was less. To put this figure in perspective, consider what impact other industries have had on the U.S. balance of payments. Close comparisons are impossible, because the estimate here for the merchant marine is more refined than any estimates that can readily be made for other industries. From 1957 through 1966 total U.S. exports of goods and services, including sales of U.S. shipping services to foreigners but excluding military grants abroad, amounted to some $329 billion; but this figure contains no adjustment for the value of foreign goods and services used to produce these exports.[16] Whatever the adjustment is, it must be small. In none of these years were total imports equal in value to more than a few percent of total U.S. output. Unless U.S. export activities are particularly heavy users of foreign inputs—as U.S. shipping is in fact—only a small adjustment is necessary to obtain the net value of U.S. exports

15. Another way of expressing the same point is to observe that if there were no maritime subsidies to pay, it would be possible to reduce taxes on the rest of the U.S. economy. A reduction in taxes would reduce costs; and a reduction in costs would promote an increase in production, some part of which would presumably be exported.

It is important to realize that this is the same point explained in the text, only expressed differently. Unless this is understood, the same adjustments may be counted twice, causing observers to understate the net impact of the U.S. merchant fleet on the nation's balance of payments. The explanation in the text is probably preferable, because it looks beyond the taxes and subsidies and focuses on the economic realities behind. The government imposes taxes on industry A and grants subsidies to industry B in order to depress industry A's demand for resources and increase industry B's; that is, in a two-industry economy, to cause resources to shift from industry A to industry B. When the subsidies are ended and the taxes are eliminated, resources presumably return from industry B to industry A; and A's output increases.

16. All the figures cited in this subsection are from U.S. Bureau of the Census, *Statistical Abstract of the United States*, various years.

from the gross value reported above. Almost surely net U.S. exports of goods and services during this period were well in excess of $250 billion.[17]

Even if we look at individual industries, we find many whose exports much exceeded in value sales to foreigners of U.S. shipping services. Agricultural exports amounted to nearly $50 billion between 1957 and 1966.[18] Exports of chemicals exceeded $19 billion, and machinery $53 billion. The list could be extended, but figures for individual industries are actually of less interest than the total for all industries. It is less important to compare the foreign exchange earnings of the merchant marine with those of this or that industry than it is to know how large they bulk in the total. The figures cited here are gross of foreign inputs.

The data above that measure the impact of the merchant marine on the nation's balance of payments include estimated foreign exchange savings through import substitution. If we wish to make some comparisons, what import savings must be attributed to the operations of such giant industries as the agricultural, automotive, and steel industries, to name but three? How much larger would the nation's import bill be if the United States were forced to do without their products? It is difficult even to imagine the country without such basic industries let alone to answer these questions; but in view of their size and output, these industries must have a massive impact on the U.S. balance of payments. Consider just the manufacturing industries. Between 1957 and 1966 the value added by all U.S. manufacturing establishments was more than $1,800 billion. A sizable fraction of this sum is reflected in the value of exports, already counted above, but there remain goods worth many hundreds of billions of dollars that were consumed at home. One could cite numerous industries whose output must have substituted for billions of dollars of imports between 1957 and 1966 and whose impact on the nation's balance of payments must therefore have been far larger than that of the shipping industry. The value added by the cigarette industry, for example, was $12.1 billion; the household furniture industry, $19.5 billion; the construction machinery equipment industry, $26.1 billion; and there are other industries that are much larger than these.

The purpose of these remarks is not to demonstrate how negligible are the activities of the U.S. merchant marine, still less how little the fleet has

17. Note well that "net exports of goods and services" are the total value of all U.S. exports less the value of foreign goods and services embodied in the exports, *not* the difference between total exports and total imports as recorded in balance of payments accounts.
18. Including exports of leaf tobacco, hides and skins, soybeans, and raw cotton.

contributed to U.S. output, but simply to indicate that in comparison with many other industries the shipping industry has had only a small impact on the nation's balance of payments. Unless there are special reasons for believing that the industry's balance of payments benefit has been disproportionately large, one must conclude that balance of payments considerations do not argue forcefully for public assistance to the merchant marine.

Distinction between Impact and Benefit

The figures above measure the impact of the U.S. merchant marine on the nation's balance of payments, but they are not necessarily an adequate measure of the balance of payments benefit of the merchant marine. The impact of the U.S. merchant fleet on the nation's balance of payments is simply the number of dollars—or number of foreign currency units expressed in dollars—that are paid each year to American shipowners instead of to foreigners in return for shipping services, less whatever expenditures are required abroad to furnish the services. In principle this is a determinate number that could with some effort be discovered.

The fleet's balance of payments benefit is more elusive. The benefit is the *value* of the fleet's impact on the U.S. balance of payments, a thing very different from the impact itself. What is it worth to the United States to decrease its balance of payments deficit by some amount? If there were no cost associated with running a deficit, no unpleasant consequences that were bound to follow, the answer would be that it was worth nothing to reduce the deficit, and the benefit of any action taken to do so would be zero, regardless of its impact. On the other hand, if the nation suffers injury from a balance of payments deficit, an action that reduces the deficit—and so mitigates the injury—is worth something, and what it is worth is spoken of as the benefit of the action.

It is easy to confuse impact and benefit and therefore important to distinguish between them. This is not always done. A recent benefit-cost analysis of the maritime program draws upon the Harbridge House study cited above in which it was estimated that the fleet's impact on the nation's balance of payments amounted to $2.2 billion during the three-year period, 1964–66.[19] Barker and Brandwein included the figure of $2.2 bil-

19. The benefit-cost analysis appears in Barker and Brandwein, *The United States Merchant Marine in National Perspective*. The Harbridge House study appears as appendix C in the same book (see note 1).

lion as the balance of payments benefit from the program, compared it with subsidy costs of several hundred million dollars during the same period, and concluded that the expenditures on the subsidy program had certainly been justified. This procedure is wholly mistaken; $2.2 billion is at most only a measure of the program's balance of payments *impact,* assuming that without the program there would have been no U.S. merchant marine. It certainly is no measure of the program's balance of payments *benefit,* and hence cannot be used to decide whether the program is worth its cost.

Balance of Payments Benefit

In practice it is almost impossible to include the balance of payments benefit of U.S. merchant shipping operations in any benefit-cost calculation. Not that merchant shipping raises peculiar problems; the same difficulties arise in evaluating the balance of payments benefit of any industry that exports a part of its product, or whose product substitutes for imports. Since this subject lies within the province of international finance, only a few comments follow concerning its relevance to the merchant marine.

All export-earning activities confer benefits on a country, if only in the form of resources obtained from foreigners for the exported goods and services. These are *not* balance of payments benefits. They have nothing directly to do with the state of a nation's balance of payments. Whether that balance is in surplus or deficit, these benefits remain the same. Furthermore, they are not fundamentally different from the benefits that residents of the exporting country enjoy by consuming the unexported balance of an industry's product and so customarily are not differentiated from them. If, for example, one portion of an industry's product is sold abroad for foreign currency worth $3 billion and the rest is sold at home for $5 billion, we say ordinarily that the value of the industry's output—the "benefits" of its operations—is $8 billion, without troubling to add that benefits worth $3 billion were obtained indirectly through an exchange of outputs with foreigners, and $5 billion obtained through direct consumption.

Accordingly it is to some extent misleading to emphasize how large a fraction of one industry's output is exported, as if these exports are mysteriously worth more than the receipts they bring. In fact they *may* be worth more—slightly more—as explained below, but in general the ordinary man is right in supposing that $3 billion of exports must be worth just $3 billion, not $2.9 billion or $3.1 billion, and that the value of an industry's total receipts, from sales at home as well as abroad, is the proper measure of the value of its output and therefore of the benefits of its operations.[20]

EFFECT ON EXCHANGE RATE. The one benefit of an industry's operations that may properly be called a balance of payments benefit is the assistance that the industry's export earnings lend to efforts to maintain the official exchange rate between the U.S. dollar and other currencies. Any U.S. industry that succeeds in exporting a part of its product, or a part of whose product substitutes for imports, creates a demand for dollars abroad, or reduces U.S. demand for foreign currencies, and so helps support the official value of the dollar in terms of other currencies. At a time when the United States was suffering sizable deficits in its balance of payments, the export earnings of the merchant marine unquestionably helped authorities maintain the value of the dollar. This is no place to consider whether the official value of the dollar should have been defended so long, until events at last forced two devaluations within fourteen months. Whether wise or not, it was the policy of this country for many years to maintain a fixed exchange rate and to use a variety of tools to defend that rate. The operations of the U.S. merchant shipping industry assisted in this effort, and the value of this assistance measures the industry's balance of payments benefit.

It is obvious how extraordinarily difficult it would be to attach any meaningful value to this benefit. What was it worth to the United States to maintain the same exchange rate between the dollar and other major currencies for so many years? And how much of this stability was due

20. One exception may be noted. In a world of fixed exchange rates and limited convertibility of currencies, it is possible for the true value of one currency in terms of another to depart from the official exchange value. It is common, for example, for developing countries to restrict the sale of their currency to support its value. Wherever this is done the foreign exchange earnings of local industries may be worth more than the official equivalent in local currency units.

If the dollar were overvalued in this manner, foreign earnings worth $3 billion at the official exchange rate might in fact be worth more than $3 billion—say $4 billion—if valued at their true marginal worth. At no time during the 1960s was the dollar overvalued in quite this way, but many other currencies were and are still. In countries with such currencies the real value of the output of export industries, such as merchant shipping, may well exceed the official value, and the difference must be accounted a real benefit that should be included in any benefit-cost calculation. Although this does not justify calling it a balance of payments benefit, since it has little to do with that accounting identity, the name apparently has been so used to stand for the difference between real and official output values.

to the earnings of the merchant marine? If public assistance to the merchant marine had ended during the 1960s, and if much of the fleet had subsequently ceased operation, what effect would the loss of the industry's export earnings have had on the value of the dollar? These questions are unanswerable; one can only speculate. The U.S. merchant marine is a relatively small industry, and its export earnings compose only a small fraction of the export earnings of all U.S. industry.[21] Its import savings must be even more negligible beside the savings of such giant industries as the automobile, steel, or textile industries. If the industry's export earnings had been lost, and if U.S. shippers had been forced to patronize foreign carriers, U.S. authorities would have found it more difficult to maintain the value of the dollar as long as they did. How would they have responded in these circumstances? Might they have devalued the dollar say three months earlier than December 1971 or February 1973? No one can say, but it is hard to imagine that the effect of the U.S. fleet's earnings could have been so important. And when the devaluations came, would they have been as little as 8 percent and 10 percent? Without the prospect of the fleet's continued earnings, the devaluations might have been marginally greater, say, 8½ and 10½ percent. Or perhaps other measures would have been taken to ward off devaluation as long as possible. Perhaps the tax on direct investment overseas would have been raised a point or two, or a small tax on travel abroad might have been imposed.

All of this is speculative. But the numbers offered here do not seem unreasonably small; if anything they probably overstate the effect of the fleet's earnings on the exchange rate of the dollar.

VALUE OF EFFECT ON EXCHANGE RATE. If it is virtually impossible to determine what effect U.S. merchant shipping operations had on the exchange value of the dollar, it is hopeless to suppose that one can measure the value of that effect. How much was it worth to the United States to maintain for so long the official value of the dollar at its former level before devaluing? How costly would it have been to have devalued by a slightly larger increment? How much would it have cost the nation to adopt other measures to compensate for the loss of the fleet's earnings? It is these questions that must be considered before any value can be placed on the balance of payments benefit of the U.S. merchant marine.

21. In the 1961–70 period sales of U.S. shipping services to foreigners were just over $7 billion. Total U.S. exports of commercial merchandise and transportation during the same period amounted to $280 billion. Data are from *Statistical Abstract of the United States,* various years.

Although they obviously cannot be answered precisely, it is apparent even with woefully inadequate information that the nation's merchant fleet could not possibly have had a very large effect on U.S. policies. Since the value of these policies is itself unknown, what can be said about the fleet's balance of payments benefit? Merely that it is a small fraction of an unknown value.

Some reputable economists even allege that it was a mistake for the government to support the dollar so long, and that it would have been less costly to have devalued sooner or by a larger fraction, or to have set the dollar free to float in response to market forces. If one accepts this view, must one conclude that far from providing a small balance of payments benefit the U.S. merchant marine was a minor liability, because it helped U.S. authorities postpone the right decision so long? Presumably not, since it would hardly be fair to blame the merchant marine for faults of judgment by public officials on subjects far removed from maritime matters. But the possibility ought to give pause to those maritime officials and their constituents who like to harp on the supposed balance of payments benefit from the industry's operations. There may be no benefit at all; and if that could ever be established one may be sure that the chorus would fall silent and nothing more would be heard about the fleet's export earnings or import savings.

Benefits with Floating Exchange Rates

The March 1973 decision of U.S. authorities to set the dollar free to float leaves the conclusions above fundamentally unchanged, although the industry's argument that merchant shipping operations create a sizable balance of payments benefit must be modified slightly. It no longer is U.S. policy to defend fixed exchange rates between the dollar and other currencies. The value of the dollar in terms of foreign currencies is in principle to be determined by supply and demand. Although nations are occasionally intervening in currency markets to influence exchange rates, the United States is not defending a particular rate for the dollar. Accordingly the nature of the balance of payments benefit, if any, that derives from merchant shipping, or from any other export industry, has changed. This benefit was previously identified as the assistance that an industry's foreign exchange earnings rendered to U.S. officials attempting to maintain a fixed exchange rate. Now that U.S. officials are no longer maintaining a fixed exchange rate, the effect of the industry's export earnings is to raise the value of the dollar slightly higher than it would otherwise be.

A small rise in the value of the dollar, considered by itself, is ordinarily beneficial to the United States. It enables Americans to buy foreign goods more cheaply and therefore makes Americans better off. To this extent the operations of the U.S. merchant shipping industry, like those of any industry that exports a part of its product, or whose product substitutes for imports, do confer a real benefit on the United States. But the rise in the value of the dollar is purchased at a price. Americans must use valuable resources to produce a product—shipping services—that fetches a lower price than the value of the resources in their best alternative use. The difference between the price that consumers pay and the value of the output that the resources could otherwise produce is the price the United States pays for cheaper imports. Whether the price is a bargain one cannot say in general; it may or may not be.[22]

Shipbuilding

The balance of payments argument for public assistance to the U.S. shipbuilding industry closely resembles the corresponding argument for public assistance to the U.S. shipping industry. Of course, the figures are different. Even if it is assumed that all the ships that the industry built during the last several years have substituted for ships that would otherwise have come from foreign yards, the U.S. shipbuilding industry has had a much smaller impact on the nation's balance of payments than the merchant marine. Correspondingly its balance of payments benefit, if any, has also been smaller. From 1967 through 1972 the value of new construction of commercial vessels in U.S. shipyards amounted to $3.0 billion.[23] During much of this period foreign ships cost little more than half the price of American ships; so industry sales may have produced foreign

22. The change to floating exchange rates probably improves the possibility of estimating what for lack of a better term may still be called the "balance of payments benefit" of the shipping industry's operations. With the help of econometric techniques it may one day be possible to estimate how much the industry's operations affect the foreign exchange value of the dollar, and how worthwhile it is to the nation to have a slightly more valuable dollar. This would be a first step—no more than that—in a benefit-cost analysis of the maritime program. But it would not be an easy exercise, especially determining how large the offsetting increase in exports would be if the resources employed in shipping were released to the rest of the economy.

23. *Report of the Commission on American Shipbuilding*, vol. 2, p. 24.

exchange savings of around $1.5 billion. This estimate is probably somewhat high. One should subtract from it the value of foreign inputs to the industry's operations, and the value of U.S. inputs that would have been purchased by foreign yards to build the ships that could have substituted for the American vessels. Exact figures are apparently not available; but the former quantity appears to be quite small, while the latter may be somewhat larger. For the purpose here it is sufficiently accurate to say that, at most, foreign exchange savings from commercial shipbuilding activity between 1967 and 1972 amounted to between $1.0 billion and $1.5 billion.

Whether the savings were $1.5 billion, $1.0 billion, or some lesser amount, the industry's balance of payments benefit was certainly much smaller. Nothing needs to be added here to the discussion above of the balance of payments impact and benefit of U.S. merchant shipping operations. Everything that was said there applies equally to the shipbuilding industry.

TOO MUCH WEIGHT has been placed on the balance of payments argument for maritime subsidies. Although the operations of the merchant shipping industry have helped improve the U.S. balance of payments, the effect has been small compared with that of other industries. The operations of the shipbuilding industry have apparently had an even smaller effect. The balance of payments benefit of the two industries' operations, which in some discussions is mistakenly identified with their balance of payments effect, has surely been smaller still. Unless some method can be found of measuring this benefit and demonstrating that it has been larger than presumed, balance of payments effects should be given little weight in judging the case for the maritime subsidies.

CHAPTER NINE

National Security and the Maritime Industries

OF THE VARIOUS justifications commonly offered for public assistance to the U.S. maritime industries, the soundest is the argument that the U.S. flag merchant marine and the U.S. shipbuilding industry contribute importantly to the nation's security. Supporters of the maritime program often allege that if assistance to these industries were ever terminated and their services were lost to the nation, the security of the United States would be gravely weakened. It is an old argument, as old as the republic, and in light of the nation's history and the important services rendered by these industries in the nation's wars it surely deserves to be taken seriously. It is unquestionably more credible than the economic arguments for maritime assistance reviewed in chapter 8 that on examination appear without merit. The national security argument commands wide respect and is obviously plausible. Indeed the principal criticism I shall make of the current program is that it is too little tailored to the security needs of the nation, notwithstanding the lip service that is continually paid to its national security objectives.

Like the economic arguments for maritime assistance, the national security argument has never to my knowledge been developed with the rigor and care that it should be.[1] The declarations of policy in all recent

1. Despite its sweeping title, the report of the Maritime Research Advisory Committee of the National Academy of Sciences is no exception to this statement (National Academy of Sciences–National Research Council, Maritime Research Advisory Committee, *The Role of the U.S. Merchant Marine in National Security,* Project WALRUS Report by the Panel on Wartime Use of the U.S. Merchant Marine [NAS–NRC, 1959]). The report is not without interest, even fifteen years later; but it is a short document of uneven depth, which the chairman of the Maritime Research Advisory Committee admitted was "primarily a new synthesis of known facts." National security was largely taken to mean military security, and much of the study is concerned with recommending measures to better prepare the U.S. merchant marine for wartime service to the nation's armed forces. Recently pro-

merchant marine acts, beginning with the Merchant Marine Act of 1920, have asserted that a U.S. flag merchant marine is necessary for the national defense; but no supporting studies have accompanied these statutes. The very competent report on the American merchant marine that the United States Maritime Commission published in 1937 included a section on the importance of shipping to the national defense.[2] The section is short and of course out of date now, but it does show that the commission regarded the fleet's contribution to national security as possibly the most important justification for a program of assistance to the U.S. merchant marine.[3] Many reports on the maritime industries have appeared since then, and most have acknowledged the importance of these industries to the national defense, especially reports that were published while memories of the Second World War were fresh in the authors' minds.[4] Lately, however, there has appeared a tendency to extol the economic benefits presumed to flow from the maritime subsidies and to pay less attention to national security. This may reflect nothing more than the modern preference for dressing up arguments in quantitative garb to enhance their authority, which often leads persons to favor a defective argument over a better one if numerical evidence is easier to find in support of it. The national security benefits of maritime assistance are more obviously difficult to quantify than the economic benefits. But if the view taken in the preceding chapter is correct, the balance of payments benefits of the maritime program—and perhaps also the employment effects—are really no easier to measure than the contribution that the program makes to national security. They only seem to be, in part because employment totals and the balance of payments—unlike national security—are concrete, measurable quantities,

ponents of commercial seapower have favored a broader definition of national security that includes protection against boycotts of U.S. commerce by foreign shipowners. The Project WALRUS report says little on this subject, and much of what it says consists of questionable generalities.

2. U.S. Maritime Commission, *Economic Survey of the American Merchant Marine* (U.S. Government Printing Office, 1937), pp. 9–13.

3. "It is obvious that national defense is an important, if not the primary, justification for the maintenance of American vessels in foreign trade" (ibid., p. 9).

4. Among recent official reports on maritime aids, perhaps the bluntest acknowledgment that national defense needs are the primary—if not only—justification for public assistance to the maritime industries appears in a letter from the Maritime Evaluation Committee to the secretary of commerce: "Government activity to promote the merchant marine derives from the national security significance of shipping" (U.S. Department of Commerce, "Maritime Resources for Security and Trade," Final Report of the Maritime Evaluation Committee to the Secretary of Commerce [U.S. Department of Commerce, 1963; processed], p. ii).

but also because the nature of these benefits has been misunderstood and they have been wrongly identified with other effects of the program. Accordingly since nothing is to be gained by focusing on the economic benefits, supporters of assistance to the maritime industries should rest their case on national security grounds and should advocate a program that really enhances the nation's security.

Even if the national security argument is presumptively sound, it must still be examined carefully to determine what kind of assistance, if any, it justifies; what volume of assistance should be provided; and what goals for the program ought to be established. Under the best conditions such an evaluation would be difficult to carry out—and probably impossible to carry out well without the full cooperation of the Department of Defense.[5]

National Security Benefits

In what ways do the maritime industries contribute to national security? Even in peacetime the shipping and shipbuilding industries perform defense services, as when American ships carry supplies for the nation's armed forces or American yards build ships for the U.S. Navy. But these are not services that justify public assistance to the maritime industries, as long as foreign flag ships are ready to carry defense cargoes and foreign shipyards are ready to build naval vessels. There exist in time of peace nearly perfect substitutes for the services of the U.S. shipping and shipbuilding industries, namely the services of foreign flag carriers and foreign shipyards; so if peace were sure to last and foreign sources of supply could be relied upon, the nation would presumably be unwilling to pay a premium for the services of the U.S. industries.[6]

5. The reader should not expect to find such a study in this chapter, which attempts only to clarify the nature of the national security benefits that may justify some maritime assistance, indicate in what ways the current maritime program does not appear to be serving the nation's security needs, and suggest some steps that might be taken to improve the program. But a strong case can be made for an official study to determine what kind of maritime program national security now requires.

6. An exception may be allowed in the case of naval procurement from U.S. shipyards. The Navy may have good reasons for preferring to build its most sophisticated vessels in American yards, despite higher U.S. construction costs. Certain features of the vessels' construction can be kept secret more easily here than abroad. And the construction of warships requires some highly specialized labor skills, which the Navy may feel the nation cannot risk losing, as might happen if orders were

The national defense value of the U.S. industries stems from the nation's uncertainty whether the services of foreign industries will always be available. In time of war the services of foreign flag carriers and foreign shipyards might be denied to the United States, forcing the nation back on its own resources for essential shipping and shipbuilding services. At the same time U.S. demand for shipping and new ships might suddenly increase, as the demand for shipping increased during the Vietnam War. If U.S. industries are more responsive to U.S. needs than foreign industries, the presence of the domestic maritime industries guarantees that a larger fraction of the additional U.S. demand for shipping or new ships would be satisfied than if the nation were dependent on foreign industries. Accordingly it may be said that the nation maintains a merchant marine and shipbuilding industry today in order to be assured of their services tomorrow, or whenever a time might come when they were the only shipping and shipbuilding industries willing or able to serve the United States.

But how large a shipping industry should the nation maintain? And how large a shipbuilding industry? What should they be like? These are essentially political questions that economic analysis alone cannot answer. The risks are so large and the uncertainty is so great that the decisions cannot be entrusted to specialists or technicians. The community must decide what level of risk it is willing to tolerate—the risk in this case being that one day the United States may have to do without the services of foreign flag carriers and foreign shipyards. This is not to say that there is no room in the community's deliberations for thoughtful, careful analyses by experts from many specialties; only that after expert testimony has been taken and all evidence has been considered the community's representatives will have to make their own decisions. No benefit-cost analyses will decide these questions for them.

The national security argument for maritime assistance divides naturally in two, one argument justifying assistance to the shipping industry, the other assistance to the shipbuilding industry. Although they have much in common, they differ enough in detail to warrant separate treatment. This book focuses on the shipping industry.[7]

---

diverted to foreign yards. In practice, however, the Navy buys nearly all its vessels from domestic shipbuilders chiefly to please Congress, not because national security demands it. Other nations—including the Soviet Union—order naval vessels from foreign shipyards, and the United States could too.

7. Partly to keep the length of this chapter within bounds, partly because the General Accounting Office is preparing a study of the shipbuilding industry (as of October 1974 the study—still untitled—had not been released), and partly because

Reliability of U.S. Flag Vessels

The fundamental assumption on which the national security argument rests is that U.S. flag vessels crewed by U.S. citizens are more responsive to the needs of this nation than vessels of foreign registry. The importance of this premise can hardly be exaggerated, for without it nothing remains of the national security argument. The essential idea is a mingling of fact and myth. The fact is that the United States, like all sovereign states, has the power to command the property of its citizens and can requisition U.S. flag vessels in a time of emergency. It enjoys no corresponding authority over most foreign flag vessels.[8] Hence the U.S. merchant marine, whether privately owned or government-owned, functions also as a national reserve fleet, available to serve the needs of the nation whenever circumstances require it. As long as the fleet exists, the commerce of the nation cannot be totally disrupted by the actions of foreign nations or the conspiracies of alien shipowners.

Here myth obtrudes. Myth suggests that foreign flag vessels are inherently unreliable, that they are owned and manned by men who are apt to subordinate their economic interests to ideology, and who if given the opportunity might hold U.S. commerce hostage for some sinister purpose, or who could be recruited to act in the service of foreign powers against the United States.[9] These ideas are seldom expressed so bluntly, and in the extreme form presented here probably command little support; but they nevertheless are often intimated in discussions of the security role of the merchant marine. In calling them mythical I do not mean that they are irrational or ridiculous, only that they rest upon belief rather than fact and are extraordinarily resistant to reasoned argument. Perhaps some foreign operators mix politics with business—some U.S. operators may

---

the national security issues that are raised by assistance to the shipping industry seem both fresher and more interesting than similar issues in regard to the shipbuilding industry, I shall focus in this chapter primarily on the national security value of the U.S. merchant marine rather than that of the shipbuilding establishment. Nonetheless, public assistance to the shipbuilding industry deserves the same careful justification on national security grounds as public assistance to the U.S. merchant marine. If the maritime aids are ever the subject of an official inquiry, both industries should be considered.

8. But see the discussion of the effective U.S. control fleet on pages 130–31.

9. Some foreign flag vessels are of course owned by U.S. citizens, individuals as well as corporations.

also—but there is no evidence that foreign carriers in general are in the habit of boycotting customers for noneconomic ends. Yet the uneasiness persists, fed by events that dramatize the dangers of depending on foreign producers for essential goods and services, such as the embargo on oil shipments to the United States that several Middle Eastern countries imposed in 1973.

The remainder of this chapter is largely devoted to examining the circumstances in which the United States might be deprived of foreign flag services. But it may be assumed that there is little danger of an effective conspiracy of foreign shipowners against U.S. customers. There have been no recent instances of such a conspiracy, and it is highly unlikely that any such effort could ever be successful. Because ships are mobile resources that can move about the globe from regions of surplus to regions of scarcity, an effective embargo would require the cooperation of shipowners around the world. Such cooperation would be very difficult to obtain in this highly fragmented industry. The number of shipowners is large, and they have little in common with one another apart from their business. Furthermore ships are reproducible assets. They can be built quickly and in large numbers, and the threat of their construction in answer to an embargo would probably undo any shipowners' association. Finally a worldwide embargo would require the assent of the governments of the most important maritime nations, nearly all of which are allies of the United States. It is inconceivable in present circumstances that their assent would be given.

Supply of Foreign Flag Carriers in Wartime

Even if the myth is untenable in its extreme form, there may still be circumstances in which foreign flag ships would stop carrying U.S. commerce. As the risk of an interruption in service increases, so does the potential value of a U.S. fleet. A war, for example, might greatly affect both the supply of foreign flag shipping available to the United States and the U.S. demand for shipping. A general war that involved the United States might cause foreign carriers to abandon service here if attacks were made on ships serving the United States. American carriers presumably would not do so, or they could be compelled not to. At the same time the U.S. demand for shipping would swell, as military supplies were moved overseas. If the United States had no fleet of its own and were dependent for shipping on foreign flag carriers, it might be squeezed between increasing demand and decreasing supply. If the squeeze were severe, the nation's security might be imperiled.

IN GENERAL CONFLICTS. On the whole, however, such a risk seems small. The threat of a general conflict is small today, surely smaller than it was twenty years ago, and probably still declining. If war did break out, the likelihood that the United States would lack allies among the world's foremost maritime nations—Japan and the nations of Western Europe— is remote. As long as it had such allies, some of which would surely be embroiled in the same conflict, the threat that foreign carriers would abandon service to the United States is simply not credible. On the contrary, service to this country would probably increase as other nations hurried to import defense materials. Of course the demand for ships would soar, as it did during the Second World War, and the current stock of vessels would no doubt be inadequate. This may argue for retaining a reserve fleet of vessels, or for maintaining a merchant fleet that is larger than the requirements of commerce alone can justify. It is also arguable that the United States should have some merchant ships of its own that would be more responsive to the directives of U.S. authorities than foreign flag vessels. But these considerations call for a much smaller U.S. fleet than would be needed if the United States really faced a withdrawal from service of many foreign flag ships that now serve the nation.

IN REGIONAL WARS. Local wars, whether involving the United States or not, would be even less likely than a large war to affect the supply of foreign flag shipping to and from the United States. The possibility that a war in which the United States took no part might depress the supply of shipping to this country may have been greater many years ago when a large fraction of the world's commerce was carried in the ships of one nation, the United Kingdom. The postwar proliferation of national fleets means, however, that in 1974 no single nation controls more than a small fraction of the world's tonnage.[10] Local conflicts involving a few countries

10. The Liberian flag merchant marine is the largest in the world. On June 30, 1974, its vessels accounted for 21.9 percent of the deadweight tonnage of all the world's oceangoing steam and motor ships of 1,000 gross tons and over. The government of Liberia exercises little control over the activities of this fleet, which is composed almost entirely of ships whose owners chose the Liberian flag of registry only because it was convenient to do so. The Japanese flag fleet is the second largest, with vessels whose deadweight tonnage aggregated 12.3 percent of the world's total. The countries with the third through the tenth largest fleets, and the size of their fleets on June 30, 1974, are: United Kingdom, 10.7 percent; Norway, 8.9 percent; Greece, 7.4 percent; United States, 3.7 percent (including merchant vessels in the National Defense Reserve Fleet); Panama, 3.6 percent; USSR, 3.6 percent; France,

could scarcely interfere much with U.S. commerce. Conflicts among the world's major maritime nations would be more disruptive; but these probably would involve the United States, in which case the remarks above apply here also.

Shipping Requirements in Wartime

Many persons undoubtedly regard an assured supply of merchant shipping as so obviously vital to military success in a war overseas that its importance requires no affirmation or discussion here. The central role played by U.S. ships in two world wars encourages this view. Nevertheless it should be pointed out that the wartime shipping needs of the armed services chiefly depend on the character and duration of the war that U.S. forces are fighting.

In General Conflicts

In a lengthy foreign conflict requiring the movement of vast amounts of matériel from one continent to another—as took place between 1940 and 1945—the importance of shipping cannot be denied. If this is the kind of war that the United States expects, the nation must not neglect its supply lines. If the chief risk is that of a short war, shipping is apt to play a much less important role in military planning. Victory will be decided in large part by the amount, location, and quality of supplies in place at the beginning of the war, not by the capability of either side to resupply its forces over an extended period. It is noteworthy that in 1974 some defense analysts in the United States believe that the chief threat of war in Europe, small as it is, is that of an intense but short conflict between the North Atlantic Treaty Organization and Warsaw Pact forces.[11] The merchant fleet of the United States would have little opportunity to affect the outcome. This is no reason to ignore shipping needs, since the expectations of experts are often wrong and the consequences of miscalculation

---

3.1 percent; and Italy, 2.9 percent. These ten fleets had 78.1 percent of the world's deadweight tonnage. (U.S. Maritime Administration, *Merchant Fleets of the World: Oceangoing Steam and Motor Ships of 1,000 Gross Tons and Over as of June 30, 1974.*)

11. For a presentation of this view and some of its implications for U.S. defense planning, see Richard D. Lawrence and Jeffrey Record, *U.S. Force Structure in NATO: An Alternative* (Brookings Institution, 1974).

would in this case be grave, but it is an additional consideration that should temper our concern over military requirements for merchant shipping.

In Regional Conflicts

If a local conflict overseas were joined by the United States, the U.S. demand for shipping would greatly increase, and the number of ships normally serving the United States would have to be augmented. Would foreign carriers come to this country's aid if the U.S. flag fleet were too small to answer the demand all by itself? There is no reason to think they would not. Foreign shipowners, like U.S. shipowners, are chiefly interested in earning profits and will generally respond to the higher freight rates that signal an increased demand for shipping services. Unless shipowners are expected to withhold their services for political reasons, there is no basis for supposing that the United States would not be able to obtain as much shipping as the country needed by bidding it away from other users.

The Vietnam War was just such a local conflict that caused a great increase in the U.S. demand for shipping; but unfortunately U.S. experience during the war provides no sure guide to the willingness of foreign carriers to make ships available to this country. U.S. law prevented foreign carriers from helping to move military supplies to Vietnam, except in a few cases when U.S. flag vessels were not available. On several occasions foreign seamen refused to sail foreign flag vessels carrying U.S. military supplies; but other times foreign carriers performed without incident. There is no evidence that the Department of Defense was displeased with the service it received from foreign carriers during the Vietnam War, though the department's experience was very limited. Certainly there was no sizable disruption of normal foreign flag service in the U.S. foreign trades during the 1960s.

Even if foreign carriers occasionally performed poorly, it would be wrong to conclude that the United States should continue to bar them from carrying U.S. military cargoes. American vessels did not always perform well either—witness the hijacking of the S.S. *Columbia Eagle*.[12] Whether American vessels in general performed better than foreign flag

12. In March 1970 two crewmen seized control of the S.S. *Columbia Eagle*, a U.S. flag vessel en route to Thailand with a cargo of munitions for U.S. forces. All crewmen, including the mutineers, were U.S. citizens. The captain was forced to sail the ship to a port in the then neutral country of Cambodia. (Reported in *New York Times,* March 16, 1970.)

vessels, and if so how much better, are questions to consider in an official study of the kind recommended below. It might be decided, for example, that U.S. vessels were slightly more reliable than foreign flag vessels. If so, and assuming for the moment that the Vietnam experience furnishes a trustworthy guide to similar conflicts in the future, the gain in reliability—that is, the improvement in security—should be weighed against the cost of maintaining a large U.S. fleet capable of moving a sizable volume of military cargoes to see whether the gain is worth the cost.

A local conflict overseas involving the United States is the most probable kind of conflict that might occur within the next several years and affect the supply of foreign flag shipping available here. If we really believe that a conflict is likely and that foreign carriers cannot be counted on to meet the nation's demand for shipping, the nation ought to be building a fleet that can be relied on. It is no secret that many of the ships that carried supplies to Vietnam have been scrapped and that it would be difficult, if not impossible, for the nation to mount a sealift in 1974 similar to the one that served U.S. forces in Vietnam in the sixties if we limited ourselves to using U.S. flag vessels. Has the nation's security been placed in jeopardy? If the answer is yes, the United States should be acquiring vessels that suit the needs of the armed services, primarily general cargo vessels capable of carrying the diverse equipment and supplies that military forces require and delivering them to poorly developed ports near the front lines of action. But the government is not doing this. The current maritime program is mostly adding vessels to the U.S. merchant marine that have little or no direct military value—large bulk carriers. These vessels may have considerable commercial value, but they could play only a minor role in support of U.S. military operations in time of war. If a person knew nothing more about the program than the kinds of vessels that are being built, he could conclude that the program was oriented toward creating a commercially viable fleet rather than creating a reserve fleet of vessels fitting the needs of the Department of Defense. His conclusion would be strengthened if he read the 1972 study on how the Defense Department could use the modern, highly productive dry cargo ships joining the U.S. merchant marine.[13] A close reading of the paper suggests that the department is accommodating its plans to the vessels that will soon compose the bulk of the U.S. dry cargo merchant fleet rather than

13. "Design Changes/Auxiliary Equipment," appendix I in "Defense Implications," pt. 3 of "Sealift Procurement and National Security (SPANS) Study," Prepared at the direction of the deputy secretary of defense (1972; processed).

acting to ensure that the fleet contains vessels that fit the department's plans.[14] This is perfectly proper as long as it is not the purpose of the maritime program to create a U.S. merchant marine adapted to the needs of the nation's armed forces. But what then is left of the national security argument?

Military Security and Economic Security

If a distinction between military and economic security is recognized, there might still be a national security argument. The fleet's contribution to military security, as expressed in its fitness for service to the nation's armed forces, is an important part of the fleet's total contribution to national security—but only a part. The U.S. merchant marine also serves the nation by carrying much U.S. commerce. Most imports, however, continue to arrive in foreign flag vessels. If this flow were ever interrupted, the nation's well-being would be in jeopardy. To the extent that U.S. flag vessels can be relied on in time of emergency more than foreign flag vessels, the creation of a U.S. flag merchant fleet that can carry a sizable fraction of the nation's commerce increases national economic security.

If the current maritime program is adding to national security, it is doing so primarily by increasing the nation's economic security rather than its military security. Some subsidies have been awarded for the construction of containerships, lighter-aboard-ship (LASH) vessels, and roll on/roll off vanships, which the Department of Defense will be able to use to supply U.S. forces during conflicts abroad. Other subsidies are helping to finance medium-sized and large tankers, which may also serve Defense Department needs. But a larger number of awards, amounting to more than half the value of all construction subsidies awarded between July 1970 and July 1974 have been for the construction of very large crude carriers (VLCCs) and liquefied natural gas (LNG) carriers.[15] If

14. We are told, for example, that "the characteristics and capabilities of merchant shipping are determined by influences largely beyond [Defense Department] control." (Ibid., p. I-4; a prefatory note cautions readers that the paper is not an official document of the department, and that not every view expressed in it is a statement of official policy.)

15. The sixty-two subsidized vessels ordered between July 1, 1970, and July 1, 1974, include three containerships, nine LASH vessels, four roll on/roll off vanships, two ore/bulk/oil carriers, twenty-two tankers, thirteen VLCCs, and nine LNG carriers. Construction subsidies of $612 million on the VLCCs and LNG carriers amounted to 58.8 percent of the value of all construction subsidies awarded during the period. (Data from U.S. Maritime Administration, Office of Shipbuilding Costs.)

such awards are justified on national security grounds, it is only because it is risky to depend on foreign flag vessels for the raw materials that the United States needs.

Risk of Interruption of Service

How risky is it? Much of the previous discussion about the effects of war on the supply of foreign flag shipping is relevant here, and also the conclusion that the risk of serious interference with U.S. commerce seems small. Although we were primarily concerned with the direct interference that a war might cause (as, for example, if carriers were frightened away from U.S. ports by threats of attack, or if hostile shipowners withheld their vessels from U.S. customers), we should also consider the disruption of U.S. commerce that might result indirectly from a conflict abroad. Wars often increase the demand for shipping and may cause shortages of vessels far from the theaters of conflict. Not even as large and important a buyer of shipping services as the United States is insulated from these effects. Perhaps this argues for entrusting a large fraction of U.S. commerce to U.S. flag vessels, which presumably could be commanded to serve the United States at a time when other carriers were hurrying elsewhere to earn higher freight rates.

The argument obviously applies to all unusual events that affect the supply of shipping: a famine in India, grain purchases by the Soviet Union, or the closing of the Suez Canal—which may be what the U.S. Maritime Commission meant when it wrote in 1937 that "the principal advantage which accrues to our foreign commerce from the possession of a domestic-flag marine is that it provides a measure of insurance against possible interruption of service."[16] The nation's economic security depends to at least some degree on continuity of shipping service, and one way to assure such continuity is to build a merchant fleet specifically to serve this nation's trade.

SIZE OF RISK. This version of the national security argument raises a number of questions. Is the likelihood of a major interruption of service large enough, and would the consequences be grave enough, to warrant the considerable expense of building and operating a U.S. flag fleet capable of carrying a sizable fraction of U.S. foreign trade? Certainly the risk of interruption seems very small. It was 1957 when U.S. flag vessels last carried as much as 15 percent by weight of all U.S. oceanborne bulk

16. *Economic Survey*, p. 5.

imports, the commodities to be carried in most of the vessels being built with construction subsidies. During much of the 1960s the fraction was only a few percent. There were abnormal events during this period that caused worldwide shortages of shipping, but the flow of U.S. commerce was never seriously interrupted. Although the future is unpredictable, it is difficult to imagine what kinds of events could cause more severe shortages of shipping during the next ten years than shippers have experienced during the past ten years.

Even if occasional shortages do occur, the United States is better able to cope with them than other nations. Shortages of shipping lead to higher freight rates; shippers who are prepared to pay high rates can generally bid away the shipping they need from other users. U.S. customers can pay higher rates than other customers and so are better protected against disruptions caused by fluctuations in the demand for shipping.[17] If there continues to be a reasonably free market in shipping—that is, if the merchant fleets of the world continue to allocate their services chiefly in response to supply and demand and are not converted into political instruments—the United States should be able at all times to purchase most of the shipping it needs from foreign operators.

EFFECT ON UNITED STATES. But if the unimaginable happened and the supply of foreign flag shipping were drastically cut, how severely would the United States be harmed? Much would depend on how long the shortage lasted. An extended shortage of shipping is too remote a possibility to waste time discussing. As long as the United States can build its own vessels, it will never want indefinitely for shipping. On the other hand a brief shortage would pose little threat. There is no really vital commodity —food, for example, or fuel—for which the United States is largely dependent on foreign suppliers. The longer a shipping shortage lasted, the

17. It is an error to suppose that the United States can at least protect itself against high freight rates by maintaining a domestic flag marine that must continue to serve U.S. trade routes, however much the demand for shipping may increase elsewhere in the world. This might ensure stable freight rates on U.S. routes. But if by remaining in the U.S. trades the vessels forgo opportunities to earn higher freight rates elsewhere, the opportunity cost of their service is high. In fact, the cost of their service is just equal to the vessels' highest potential earnings elsewhere (less any increase in operating costs that they would have to pay). Accordingly the United States would not be protected from higher freight rates; it would "pay" them anyway in the form of forgone earnings by its captive fleet.

In practice of course the United States would probably pay the higher rates explicitly. It is naive to imagine that U.S. flag carriers could be prevented for long from increasing their rates if rates elsewhere increased considerably.

more disruptive it would be; a shortage of intermediate duration might embarrass the nation the most: long enough for inventories of imported materials to be depleted, but too short for extensive adjustments to be made within the economy and substitutes for scarce materials to be developed, or for a fleet to be built to replace absent carriers.

Still, the United States is much less dependent on imports of raw materials than other nations and better able to endure interruptions in supply. Although petroleum imports account each year for a constantly increasing fraction of total U.S. petroleum consumption, domestic wells remain the source of most of the nation's supply. The story is much the same with many other important commodities. Only a few that are important in the life of the nation must largely be imported from overseas—tin and bauxite are examples. As long as the United States can meet most of its requirements from its own resources, it has little to fear from a temporary reduction in imports. This fact must be considered in judging how much this nation should spend to ensure a more secure system of delivery of imported materials.

Precautionary Measures

Suppose that the government of the United States decided that the risk is not small that a shortage of foreign flag shipping may one day interrupt imports; that the effects of an interruption, even if it were brief, might be serious; and that protective preparations ought to be made. Constructing a U.S. flag fleet to carry much of our commerce is one action that the nation might take to ensure that at least part of its commerce would continue to move. But it should not be forgotten that other actions might be taken that could protect the nation almost as effectively—or more effectively—and at lower cost. To mention one, the nation might create stockpiles of vital materials. The United States followed this policy for many years after the Second World War, but lately has been reducing many of its stockpiles, apparently because authorities have decided that the quantities in storage are greatly in excess of any conceivable need for them. If ever it were decided that foreign flag services were unreliable, the reductions could be halted and stockpiles could once again be increased. Since the chief risk, such as it is, is not that U.S. commerce would be stopped for long but that it might suffer a short interruption, the fact that stockpiles are exhaustible resources is not a serious objection to relying on them in emergencies.

Effective United States Control Fleet

Not all foreign flag vessels are deemed by the U.S. government to be equally unreliable in times of emergency. A limited number are in the "effective United States control fleet"—ships of foreign registry over which U.S. authorities believe they exercise effective control. The phrase is a technical one and denotes ships that meet three conditions: (1) U.S. citizens or corporations have more than half the ownership; (2) the ship was transferred from U.S. to foreign registry under a Maritime Administration contract or is insured with the U.S. government under a war risk insurance contract; and (3) the ship is registered under the flag of Panama, Liberia, or Honduras. The owners of these vessels have agreed to place the ships under U.S. registry in time of war, and the governments of Panama, Liberia, and Honduras have publicly stated that they will raise no objections to the transfer of registry. According to U.S. authorities these vessels are available in times of emergency.

On December 31, 1973, the effective United States control fleet numbered 457 vessels. Only twenty-six vessels were general cargo carriers (freighters and refrigerated cargo ships). The rest were tankers and dry bulk carriers, except for nine passenger ships. The fleet contains so few general cargo vessels that it could play only a small role in supplying U.S. forces overseas. Hence its contribution to U.S. military security, strictly defined, is probably small. On the other hand it has enough tankers and dry bulk carriers—many more than the U.S. flag fleet—to contribute importantly to U.S. economic security, assuming that in practice it really is under effective U.S. control and that the ships really could be requisitioned by the U.S. government if they ever were needed.

This last assumption has been vigorously denied by spokesmen for U.S. maritime interests who maintain that any fleet under foreign registry and manned by foreign crews is less reliable than U.S. flag vessels manned by U.S. citizens. It is impossible to say whether their doubts are warranted.[18]

18. It is worthwhile remarking, however, that the United Kingdom, whose security depends far more than ours on the uninterrupted flow of imports, has always allowed its ships to be crewed by foreigners, although it has required that certain officers on the ships must be British. It appears that in 1966 non-Europeans (chiefly Indians) may have filled as many as one-third of the positions that they were eligible for aboard U.K. ships. (*Committee of Inquiry into Shipping: Report,* Cmnd. 4337 [London: Her Majesty's Stationery Office, 1970], pp. 222–23.) Apparently it has never been suggested that their employment threatened the security of the United Kingdom.

The United States has never tested its effective control by requisitioning these vessels.[19] Until it does, doubts must remain whether the vessels actually will respond to U.S. commands. Furthermore there appears to be some uncertainty whether U.S. claims of jurisdiction over American-owned foreign flag vessels are soundly based in international law.[20] But it cannot be stressed too much that all discussions of national security are inevitably colored by doubt and uncertainty; that the national security argument itself rests on uncertain foundations; that the dangers that the nation seeks protection from are uncertain dangers; and that no matter what we do, we cannot escape risk entirely. The fact that the effective United States control fleet is not in some sense absolutely reliable in no way disqualifies U.S. officials from taking account of it in their defense planning. It means at most that official estimates of the fleet's contribution to the nation's security must be discounted below the contribution that the same fleet would make if it were currently registered under the U.S. flag. Perhaps this has been done. The Department of Defense studied the matter several years ago and apparently decided that the effective control fleet was sufficiently reliable to be included in U.S. defense planning. On the department's authority the fleet may be said to increase the nation's economic security.

Current Maritime Program

The question remains whether the current U.S. maritime program is increasing the nation's economic security. The answer offered here is that it is, but probably not by much. It must be assumed that U.S. flag vessels are more reliable than foreign flag vessels, otherwise the national security argument, ever fragile, crumbles away. With that assumption, it follows that *other things being equal* the larger the U.S. merchant marine, the more secure the nation. But things are rarely that simple and a few qualifying remarks must be added.

Commercial Orientation of Program

In the first place, it is strictly improper to measure changes in national security by looking only at the expenditure side of accounts. Adding

19. But during the Second World War all American-owned vessels under Panamanian and Honduran registry were assimilated into the U.S. war effort.
20. See "How Effective Is U.S. Control over American Owned Foreign Flag Vessels?" appendix G, annex A, in "Defense Implications," pt. 3 of the SPANS study.

vessels to the merchant marine is costly. The construction program consumes resources that could find other uses (unless in its absence the resources would lie idle). The security value of these other uses should be measured and compared with the value of the additional vessels. Only then can one judge whether the program on balance is improving national security. But obviously this cannot be done. No one is sure how the resources that the program consumes would otherwise be used. A thoughtful guess would be that on balance the construction and operating programs do enhance national security.

Even if the programs do increase the nation's security, they might increase it more if their character were changed. The mix of vessels that are under construction reflects the commercial orientation of the shipbuilding program. The vessels being built are those whose prospects for commercial success are brightest. This is inevitable, given the constraints that the Maritime Administration is operating under. It cannot subsidize the construction of vessels that operators are unwilling to buy; and operators will only buy ships that meet the requirements of their trade. Thus among the ships that have recently been built or are being built with construction subsidies are several supersize tankers that are too large to call at any U.S. port. They may have to trade between foreign countries, carrying oil, for example, from the Persian Gulf to Western Europe.[21] It strains credulity to say that these vessels will add anything to U.S. security. They are being built chiefly because at the time contracts were let they were the most attractive vessels that shipowners wanted.

It is possible to say more: that some of the vessels under construction not only will add nothing to U.S. security but may actually detract from it. Consider the liquefied natural gas carriers. If these vessels enter service carrying gas from, say, Algeria to the eastern United States, will U.S. security be improved? If the only alternative were to carry the gas in foreign flag vessels, perhaps it might be. But if one considers the alternative of exploiting untapped domestic reserves instead of importing the gas, must one not conclude that these vessels lessen U.S. security?[22] What is the point of adding minimally to the safety of the pipeline when the spigot at the source is still so vulnerable?[23]

21. In May 1974 the T.T. *Brooklyn,* the first U.S. supertanker built with a subsidy, was reported in service between North Africa and the Netherlands (*Christian Science Monitor,* May 14, 1974).

22. It is not a satisfactory reply to say that the vessels themselves do not lessen U.S. security; rather their employment does. Once the vessels are built the political pressure for putting them to use may be irresistible.

23. The maritime program illustrates the myopia of policymakers who become

Most of the vessels under construction will be able to serve the U.S. trades; but there is no certainty that they actually will. When the President's maritime program was sent to Congress in 1970, the Maritime Administration proposed that vessels built with construction subsidies should be subject to administrative restrictions upon the trades they might serve. This provision was deleted from the bill before it was enacted, principally it seems because operators argued that such restrictions would greatly reduce the flexibility they needed to operate the new vessels successfully. Their objections were reasonable and illustrate neatly how the requirements of security can conflict with the requirements of commerce. In the highly competitive business of shipping, operators must be able to move their ships into the trades where they earn the highest return, otherwise their livelihood may be jeopardized. Yet, as observed earlier, one of the reasons for maintaining a U.S. flag fleet is to protect U.S. commerce from shortages of shipping caused by increases in demand elsewhere in the world. Inasmuch as the owners of vessels built with construction subsidies are not bound to serve U.S. commerce, not even this advantage may be realized.

The preference in the construction program for vessels that are commercially attractive may be one of the chief flaws in the program, if it is judged by its contribution to national security. But it would be wrong to infer that vessels whose commercial promise is brightest are necessarily those that contribute the least to the nation's security. That may not be the case at all. The point is rather that the goal of building a commercially viable fleet—a fleet that can compete in world markets with the ships of other nations—is not the same as the goal of building a fleet that adds greatly to the nation's security.

Conflicting Interests of Defense and Commerce

The chief reason of course why the construction program serves the security requirements of the nation so imperfectly is that it is entrusted

---

preoccupied with optimizing the performance of some subsystem within a larger system whose total performance is far from optimal. The question whether the United States should depend on foreign sources for much of the oil and gas it needs touches U.S. security far more intimately than the minor question of how foreign oil and gas should be carried here. Until recently, however, the former question seems to have attracted less attention than the latter.

It is not fair of course to blame this confusion of priorities wholly on maritime officials. Much of the fault lies with policymakers at higher levels, perhaps in the U.S. Office of Management and Budget, who have failed to ensure that the goals of the maritime program are consonant with other national objectives.

to an agency with a quite different mission from that of the Defense Department. The Maritime Administration is in the Department of Commerce and its policies reflect the largely commercial interests of that department. Accordingly no one should be surprised that programs designed by the Maritime Administration comport poorly with the requirements of another government department whose responsibilities are much different. It should be emphasized that poor communications are not only to blame, and that the program is unlikely to be improved by such palliative measures as ensuring that the views of the Department of Defense receive a hearing by maritime officials or even exhorting the Maritime Administration to pay more heed to national security objectives. The Maritime Administration will not dance to the Defense Department's tune, even if it perceives the department's needs perfectly, as long as it imagines that the nation's commerce requires a strong merchant fleet or that balance of payments considerations argue for the fleet's expansion.

Another consequence of lodging responsibility for the maritime program outside the Department of Defense is that it creates a tendency to spend too much on maritime aids. Because the costs of maritime assistance appear in the budget of the Maritime Administration instead of in that of the Defense Department, neither agency has an incentive to balance construction subsidies against other means of achieving national security objectives in the maritime area. On the contrary, both agencies have every incentive to press for more maritime assistance, so long as additional ships add something to the nation's security, no matter how little. No amount of consultation between the agencies will alleviate this problem. Even today proponents of the maritime program are often accommodated when they ask the Department of Defense to endorse their spending proposals. Why should the department refuse, if a single extra vessel adds one iota to the nation's security?

The Defense Department's complaisance should not be exaggerated. The department will not endorse every scheme, no matter how bizarre or unpromising, that advocates of commercial seapower put forward. In 1962 Secretary of Defense Robert S. McNamara made it clear that he would not follow the example of his predecessors and support an expansion of the subsidy program.[24] But McNamara was an unusual man, gifted

24. "I do not wish to leave the impression that we have no requirement for merchant shipping. Obviously we do. But rather I do not wish to overstate the military requirement, thereby providing an umbrella under which a huge ship construction program for the merchant marine can be justified." (Robert S. McNamara,

with a superior understanding of how the nation's security hinged on the efficient use of all U.S. resources, not only those that the Defense Department commanded. The nation's resources were too dear to be squandered; waste elsewhere in the economy could mean that fewer resources would be available for national defense. It cannot be assumed that such men will always be in charge of the Defense Department. Even when they are, their influence is limited. For example, during McNamara's tenure other officials in the department and in the Navy continued to press for a larger U.S. merchant fleet. Lately the Defense Department has resumed its support for a large merchant shipbuilding program, but apparently has done little to see that the Maritime Administration builds ships tailored to the department's requirements.[25]

If increases in spending on maritime programs were borne by the Department of Defense, if defense officials were forced to defend the national security value of the programs as an item in their own budget, and if the same officials understood that giving more aid to the maritime industries would leave less money for other defense programs, it is likely that spokesmen for the department would weigh their needs more carefully and would be less prone to endorse maritime projects of dubious defense value. Defense officials seldom condition their support for maritime assistance on the willingness of others to pay the cost, but equally seldom are they asked whether they would persist in their support if funds for the program came from the Defense Department budget.[26] It is just this question that they have to be asked if the nation is to avoid wasting money on maritime programs that add little or nothing to the nation's security.

---

in *Review of Merchant Marine Policy,* Hearings before the House Committee on Merchant Marine and Fisheries, 87 Cong. 2 sess. [1962], p. 107; quoted in Samuel A. Lawrence, *United States Merchant Shipping Policies and Politics* [Brookings Institution, 1966], p. 107). It should be noted that even before McNamara assumed office the Department of Defense had begun estimating its probable needs for merchant shipping more conservatively and was no longer so uncritically supporting plans to expand the U.S. merchant fleet (Lawrence, *U.S. Merchant Shipping,* pp. 106–07).

25. No representative of the Defense Department or the Navy testified in hearings on the House and Senate bills that became the Merchant Marine Act of 1970. Brief communications from the secretary of defense and the under secretary of the navy affirmed the department's support "for building and maintaining a strong and economically viable U.S. Merchant Marine" (*President's Maritime Program,* Hearings before the Subcommittee on Merchant Marine of the House Committee on Merchant Marine and Fisheries, 91 Cong. 2 sess. [1970], pt. 2, pp. 279–80).

26. Sometimes, however, they volunteer the answer. (See the remark of the under secretary of the navy quoted above, p. 34, note 26.)

136 BREAD UPON THE WATERS

The root of the problem is that it is impracticable to estimate the national security value of a maritime program in dollars and cents. The benefits of the program are too uncertain and too diffuse to measure directly. The same difficulty plagues all analyses of defense spending, no matter what form the spending takes. But it is often possible to compare two programs and decide which one purchases more security for the same expenditure of funds. If we wish to spend money on the nation's security, we ought to consider whether the money should be spent on a maritime program or whether more security could be purchased by spending the money another way. In order to decide, we must make comparisons; but today the maritime program is protected from such comparisons and thus from the careful scrutiny the program deserves. The Defense Department continues to support increases in maritime spending, knowing that none of the money will come from its programs. The Maritime Administration presses for larger subsidies, and no one is interested enough to point out that the money it asks for might be spent more effectively on other defense programs.[27]

The same tendency to overstate the Defense Department's requirements for U.S. flag merchant shipping is apt to color any advice the department would give to an independent body investigating the national security role of the U.S. merchant marine. Unless such a group were aware of this tendency it might accept the department's recommendations uncritically and propose a level of maritime spending greater than is necessary to satisfy the nation's security needs.

There is no easy way of solving this problem without creating others in turn. Removing responsibility for the maritime programs from the Department of Commerce to the Department of Defense is a drastic measure that could be justified only if the sole reason for giving assistance to the maritime industries is to maintain a military reserve for wartime employment. If there are other reasons for assisting these industries—if for example the nation's economic security must be safeguarded by fostering a domestic marine that can carry much of this nation's peacetime commerce—it would be unwise to place responsibility for the program in a department with such narrow objectives. A less radical change would

27. It is not necessary of course that any reduction in maritime spending should be matched by an increase in another form of defense spending. If the Defense Department were suddenly obliged to spend $200 million annually in support of the U.S. merchant marine, it might suddenly discover that a much smaller annual expenditure would enable it to accomplish its mission satisfactorily.

leave the administration of the maritime program with the Department of Commerce but provide that a specified fraction of maritime expenditures should be financed from Defense Department appropriations. This innovation presumably would encourage the Defense Department to examine more carefully its needs for merchant shipping and explore less costly alternatives that might be just as effective. It is probably premature, however, to propose such substantial changes before the objectives of the maritime program have been better defined. After we sort out the reasons why the nation should maintain a domestic merchant marine and a shipbuilding industry, we can decide how far to regard maritime spending as a defense expenditure that properly belongs in the budget of the Defense Department. Until then the most we can hope for is that the Office of Management and Budget will exercise its responsibilities more vigorously during the budget-making process and urge the Department of Defense to evaluate its needs as realistically as possible, meanwhile insisting that the Maritime Administration should justify on national security grounds ,all requests for funds for maritime assistance.

IN CONCLUSION, national security considerations may provide an authentic justification for a program of assistance to the U.S. maritime industries. But the program should be designed expressly to serve the nation's security requirements. It should be preceded by an official study of the dangers to the nation from relying on foreign suppliers for its shipping needs. The proper place to carry out such a study is within the government, where it might be done by an official commission constituted for the purpose and composed predominantly of persons not closely associated with maritime or defense interests. Experience dictates that the study should not be entrusted to any agency much involved in maritime affairs or to the Department of Defense, although the experience of these organizations and the data they collect would provide the basis for much of the work that would have to be done. Action might then be taken to moderate the risks to national security by creating and maintaining a merchant marine of appropriate size and suitable characteristics. The current maritime program, which has as its goal the creation of a U.S. merchant fleet that will carry a much larger share of U.S. foreign commerce than the fleet carries now, may incidentally be increasing the nation's security. It would increase security more, however, and probably at lower cost if it were turned away from its purely commercial objectives and were tailored explicitly to the security needs of the nation.

CHAPTER TEN

Summing Up

THIS CHAPTER SUMMARIZES the most important points that have been made above. The costs of the maritime aids are reviewed first. A discussion follows of several economic arguments that are often advanced for these aids. The national security goals of the maritime program are considered next. The chapter concludes by recommending that an official study should be undertaken to define the proper objectives of federal maritime assistance and to determine how the current program should be altered to serve the nation better.

Principal Maritime Aids

Of the many federal aids for the U.S. maritime industries described in this book, the operating differential subsidy has been among the most expensive. The government has been paying operating subsidies to selected U.S. flag steamship companies since 1936. By fiscal year 1973 they had cost over $3.6 billion, more than half of which had been paid out since 1962. Hovering around the $200-million-a-year mark for the last decade, they now appear to be on the rise again in 1974 and may soon exceed $250 million a year.

Operating subsidies are given to offset the difference between the high costs paid by U.S. flag operators and the lower costs of their foreign competitors. Most of the difference is attributable to the higher wages received by crews aboard U.S. vessels, and so most of the subsidy is paid in respect of wages. In 1969 the federal government paid about 67 cents of every dollar of wages aboard U.S. cargo vessels in subsidized service, and the government's share has probably not declined much since. Subsidy payments covered nearly a quarter of the operating expenses of all such vessels, and provided operators with nearly a fifth of their revenues.

Another important aid to the maritime industries is the construction differential subsidy. Unlike the operating subsidy the construction subsidy is designed to assist shipbuilders rather than shipowners: to increase the demand for U.S.–built vessels by lowering their prices to those of similar vessels built in a foreign shipyard. During most of the postwar years the prices of ships built in this country have been nearly double—sometimes more than double—the prices of ships built abroad. The government has, in fact, invested as much money in the new vessels as the buyers themselves.

Between 1936 and fiscal year 1973, construction subsidy payments totaled over $1.8 billion. Most of this sum has been paid since 1957 when a major construction program began. With the announced goal in 1970 of adding the equivalent of 300 new "standard size" vessels to the U.S. merchant fleet by the early 1980s, construction subsidy costs during the next decade threaten to exceed $3 billion.

Although the cabotage laws of the United States confer no subsidies in the conventional sense on any party and involve no disbursements from the public treasury, they are of considerable benefit to the maritime industries and belong in any account of the public aids these industries receive. The cabotage laws restrict the carriage of goods in the nation's domestic oceanborne commerce to vessels built and registered in the United States. The costs of this protection are sizable. I estimate that between 1950 and 1970 private shipowners were forced to pay nearly $1 billion more for the vessels they needed in the domestic trades than they would have paid for similar vessels from foreign shipyards. More costly still has been the requirement that vessels in the domestic trades must sail under the U.S. flag. Between 1950 and 1970 this added about $2 billion to shipping costs. Precisely who has paid these $3 billion of costs it is difficult to say, but it has probably been the consumers of the goods carried in these ships.

The fourth subsidy described in this book is administered through the federal tax system. The tax subsidies to the maritime industries constitute an extraordinary form of public assistance, available to no other industry. The program functions much like a loan program, with the federal government granting qualified shipowners the use of tax money to buy ships and equipment from U.S. producers. The owners pay no interest for their use of the money, and no date is set when repayment is due. Under certain conditions the subsidy is substantially equivalent to an exemption from income tax of a part of shipowners' earnings.

Before 1950 the value of the tax subsidies was greater even than the operating subsidy payments to shipowners. Recently, however, their value has fallen. I estimate that between 1936 and the end of 1970 the maritime tax subsidies cost the federal government about $350 million. During the past several years their annual cost can hardly have exceeded $10 million. Legislation in 1970 greatly broadened the conditions under which the subsidy can be claimed. Within the next few years the annual cost should increase appreciably, possibly to more than $50 million.

The U.S. cargo preference laws have recently been the most important form of federal maritime assistance. These laws require that at least 50 percent—and in some cases 100 percent—of certain classes of cargo, called "government-impelled cargo," must be carried aboard U.S. flag vessels. The U.S. merchant fleet has become heavily dependent on preference shipments for the bulk of its business. Between 1964 and 1969, for example, preference cargoes totaled about 7 percent by weight of all U.S. oceanborne exports and imports, but composed more than half of all exports and imports carried by U.S. vessels.

The reservation of one-half of the preference trade to U.S. vessels confers a sizable benefit upon the U.S. merchant marine. Because U.S. flag vessels cost roughly twice as much to operate as foreign flag ships, customers must often pay premium rates to ship their cargoes aboard U.S. vessels. I estimate that between 1952 and 1972 the cargo preference laws added around $5 billion to taxpayers' costs, making these laws the most expensive form of maritime assistance in recent U.S. history.

Economic Rationale for Assistance

Although the federal government aids the maritime industries principally because they are thought to be essential to the nation's security, some champions of maritime assistance have argued that there are also sound economic reasons for continuing this support. They attribute a sizable increase in economic activity to the maritime aids, specifically to the large new shipbuilding program, but by inference to other maritime aids also. They compute the share of new output that will flow to the government as additional taxes, observe that this sum may approach the total of public expenditures on the shipbuilding program, and conclude that therefore the program is nearly costless—or at least much less costly than budgetary figures indicate.

As usually formulated this argument is not very credible. Whatever force it has depends largely on the assumption that the resources employed in the shipping and shipbuilding industries would lie idle in the absence of the maritime aids; otherwise we must debit the output of these resources in alternative employment against their output in the maritime industries to determine what the net gain in product has been. The scanty evidence available suggests that U.S. shipbuilders have difficulty securing and retaining the labor they need to build all the merchant ships their customers have ordered, hence that their activity, like that of most enterprises, reduces output elsewhere in the economy.

It is also wrong to suppose that the larger the amount of new output that the government takes in additional taxes, the less costly the program. The cost of the program is measured only by the resources it uses, not by the government's receipts or expenditures.

Another popular argument for the maritime aids stresses the balance of payments benefit from U.S. shipping and shipbuilding activities. We are told that because the entire output of these industries either is exported or replaces imports, the operations of the merchant marine and domestic shipyards have an important impact on the nation's balance of payments. The foreign exchange these industries earn is a valuable bonus that justifies the assistance they receive.

This argument also is defective. The term "balance of payments benefit" evidently means something other than an industry's export earnings, since these already are included in the value of the industry's product and would therefore be counted twice if they were added again to the benefits of the industry's operations. In a world of fixed exchange rates, the balance of payments benefit presumably is the support an industry's earnings give to the exchange value of a nation's currency, if other forces are eroding it. If the export earnings of the maritime industries helped lessen the need for drastic measures to protect the value of the dollar, or helped postpone devaluation or reduced the size of the devaluation that eventually came, it is fair to credit these industries with a balance of payments benefit (assuming, as public authorities did, that it was desirable to postpone devaluation, and when the dollar had to be devalued, to devalue it as little as possible). But this benefit must have been very small, much smaller certainly than the value of the export earnings or import savings of either industry. The U.S. maritime industries are dwarfs in the American economy. Their effect on the U.S. balance of payments is much smaller than that of many other industries. Accordingly if the United States benefited by forestalling devaluation as long as possible, and if American industry deserves a part of the credit for the delay, the share of this credit that may be apportioned to the maritime industries must be small. Or to put it another way, if federal subsidies were to be paid to every industry whose operations produced as large a balance of payments benefit as that produced by the operations of the maritime industries, dozens of industries would immediately be entitled to public assistance.

The ending of fixed exchange rates between the dollar and other currencies in March 1973 does not affect the argument. The operations of the U.S. shipping and shipbuilding industries now have the effect of slightly increasing the value of the dollar in terms of other currencies, whereas previously they helped authorities resist a devaluation of the dollar. The difference is unimportant here, since the value of either effect—the balance of payments benefit—presumably is the same. And so we are still justified in saying that the balance of payments argument should be put aside and the case for the maritime aids should rest where it ought to have been all the time: on the role the maritime industries play in support of the nation's economic and military security.

National Security Argument

The national security argument contains the soundest justification for a program of public assistance to the U.S. maritime industries. The core of the argument is that these industries contribute importantly to the nation's security by reducing U.S. dependence on foreign suppliers for ships and shipping services. Spokesmen for the industries like to assure us that although foreign suppliers are ordinarily reliable, the risk that one day they may suddenly withdraw from U.S. markets, or that their services may somehow be forcibly withheld from the nation, makes it imperative for the United States to maintain its own maritime industries. The industries need not be large enough to serve all the nation's normal maritime needs, but they should be able to serve a sizable fraction of them, in order to mitigate the most serious effects of a withdrawal from service by foreign suppliers.

The national security argument will always be largely intuitive, owing to the extreme difficulty of measuring the risks that a U.S. flag fleet is intended to forestall. That the risk of an interruption in foreign flag service is difficult to estimate is no reason to reject the argument. The nation's need for ships has been proved during several wars, when the United States had to rely on its own resources to procure the shipping it needed. But this difficulty aggravates the task of deciding what the nation should do to protect itself. Certainly the first step should be to identify the circumstances in which an interruption in service is most likely to happen. Although one sometimes hears remarks about the inherent unreliability of foreign flag vessels and the possibility of shipowners conspiring to withhold their services from U.S. customers, or being directed to do so by their countries of registry, the greater danger to continuity of service is the threat of war, with all its disruptive consequences. A war involving the United States might greatly reduce the amount of foreign flag shipping available here, at the same time as the U.S. demand for shipping was suddenly increasing. If the Department of Defense were unable to obtain the shipping it needed, the nation's security would clearly be threatened. To protect the nation against this risk, it may be necessary to maintain a U.S. flag merchant marine capable of meeting at least part of the probable shipping needs of the Defense Department. In filling this role—essentially that of a military reserve—the fleet may correctly be said to be increasing the nation's military security.

But sometimes a larger role is claimed for the fleet. We sometimes are told that much of the nation's overseas commerce must move in U.S. flag vessels if the nation's security is to be protected. Exactly how the nation's security is threatened when foreign flag vessels carry our commerce has never been properly explained; but apparently a number of ideas are mingled, including the thought that foreign carriers may be less responsive to the needs of U.S. customers than U.S. carriers, or that they are apt to abandon service to the United States on slighter pretexts, or even that if given the opportunity their owners might conspire to hold U.S. commerce hostage for some sinister purpose. Accordingly the security of the nation —in this case its economic security—is increased when U.S. trade is entrusted to U.S. flag vessels.

However reasonable this argument may seem at a time when commercial relations between nations are becoming more acrimonious, it will not withstand scrutiny. There is no danger today that the world's shipowners could effectively combine to boycott a single nation's commerce— especially the commerce of the world's largest trading nation. The merchant shipping industry is too fragmented; the industry's resources are too mobile; ships are too easily built. Moreover most of the major maritime nations are allies of the United States and their governments would be sure to disapprove participation by their nationals in any such embargo. If one distant day circumstances change and the possibility of a shipping boycott against this country no longer seems fanciful, there will be ample time to decide how the United States ought to respond and to consider less costly—and possibly more effective—ways of meeting the threat than expanding the U.S. flag merchant marine.

Conclusion

What is chiefly wrong with the current maritime program is that its goal of creating a competitive U.S. flag fleet is the wrong goal. Why is it in the interest of this nation to spend public funds on the merchant marine, if it is not to increase the nation's security? We ought to recognize this goal explicitly and redesign the program accordingly, rather than persist in policies that increase national security only incidentally. It would be necessary of course to distinguish economic security from military security, and to realize that the two may not be served equally by one program. In my opinion, and for the reasons explained earlier, the economic security of the United States is not much jeopardized now by our reliance on foreign flag vessels to move the bulk of our foreign commerce.

The nation needs a careful and dispassionate examination of the national security argument by a public body having the power to summon evidence from all quarters of the government. A commission constituted especially for the purpose and composed of men without prior experience in maritime affairs might be entrusted with this task. They should be instructed to evaluate even the basic premises underlying the national security argument and to draw whatever conclusions for maritime policy that their study warrants. They should determine whether reasons of security require that any portion of the nation's peacetime foreign commerce should travel aboard U.S. flag vessels; and if they find such reasons, should justify them scrupulously. They should investigate whether the safety of the nation in a future conflict might depend on the availability of adequate shipping and should weigh the risk of relying for that shipping on foreign carriers. They should prepare an inventory of the nation's maritime resources and should tell us whether the nation's safety requires that these resources be augmented. Very probably the Merchant Marine Act will have to be amended. The emphasis in the maritime program may shift from construction subsidies back to operating subsidies. The program will no doubt be smaller. But the result should be a program that more closely fits the needs of the United States, and that might even contribute substantially to the security of the nation.

Preference Costs of Military Shipments

THIS APPENDIX contains a fuller explanation than appears in chapter 7 of how I estimated the costs of cargo preference in connection with the shipment of military cargoes. By the costs of cargo preference, I mean the difference between the costs that the Military Sealift Command (MSC)[1] paid for the shipment of cargoes aboard privately owned U.S. flag vessels and the costs the command would have paid if the cargoes had moved aboard foreign flag vessels. I include also the extra costs of chartering U.S. flag vessels, but not the costs of engaging U.S. operators to sail government-owned vessels under the direction of the command.

Perhaps not all of this difference should be called the costs of cargo preference, since it is plausible to suppose that at least some cargoes would have continued to move aboard American vessels even in the absence of the preference laws. The costs of using American vessels would describe the figure more accurately, though even this description too would have to be qualified. But it is a reasonable presumption that a large part of these costs would not have been incurred if the preference laws had not been in force.

Between 1952 and 1966 the majority of commercial payments by the Military Sealift Command were made for the purchase of space aboard U.S. flag liners at terms agreed on in special shipping contracts.[2] These contracts between the MSC and private liner companies established the freight rates that the command agreed to pay for the carriage of its cargoes. Uniform rates were agreed on with all carriers serving the same trade. Cargoes were allocated among lines in proportion to their sailings.

The first shipping contracts were negotiated in 1950. Thereafter freight rates were occasionally raised when carriers could persuade the command

---

1. I use this name throughout this appendix, despite the fact that before 1970 this department was known as the Military Sea Transportation Service.
2. For more detail concerning the procedures that the command followed to purchase space aboard U.S. flag liners, see U.S. Department of Defense, "Understanding the Current Systems," pt. 1 of "Sealift Procurement and National Security (SPANS) Study," Prepared at the direction of the deputy secretary of defense (1972; processed), pp. 2–21.

that their operating costs had increased. The command twice negotiated decreases in rates when it appeared that commercial rates had fallen below military rates. In 1964 the MSC conducted a study of commercial and military freight rates, from which it concluded that the rates it was paying under its shipping contracts were excessive. There followed a series of meetings between the command and the carriers, proposals for new methods of procuring shipping space, the entry of a new steamship operator on the North Atlantic route that was willing to carry military cargoes at lower rates than the command had been paying, and a sharp reduction in rates by the established carriers to meet the new competition. At length the Department of Defense, over the objections of the operators, decided to scrap the existing method of procuring ocean transportation and substitute another that promoted competition for military cargoes and promised lower costs for the MSC.

The method of procurement that the command instituted in 1966 has been followed, with modifications, ever since.[3] Freight rates are set not by negotiation but by a procedure closely akin to competitive bidding. Toward the end of each fiscal year the command requests U.S. liner companies to propose the rates that the companies are willing to offer the MSC during the next fiscal year. On the basis of these tenders, as modified by negotiation between the command and the companies, the command assigns positions to the companies, the highest positions corresponding to the lowest rates. The command contracts with the operators to offer them cargoes in the order of their position. Limits are placed on the share of cargo moving over each route that any single company may carry, to prevent it from monopolizing traffic. At first no line was obliged by its contract to furnish any services; but that has recently been changed.[4] In the event that a line refuses a shipment or is unable to offer a sailing at the time the goods must move, the command offers the shipment to the next line in position, and if refused again, to the line after that, until the cargo finds a carrier.

3. But only for transportation to foreign destinations. The command still procures transportation on domestic routes, including the noncontiguous trades, by negotiated contract. Traffic to foreign destinations is much the larger of the two. In fiscal 1972, for example, the command purchased $267.4 million of transportation under the new shipping agreements, and just $21.1 million under the old shipping contracts. (See U.S. Navy, Military Sealift Command, *Financial and Statistical Report,* pts. 1 and 2, published quarterly.)

4. The command now insists that the operators offering the lowest freight rates on a few specified routes must carry a minimum of 20 percent or 25 percent of all military cargoes moving on those routes.

The reason for recalling this history is to explain how it happened that after 1966 freight rates for the movement of military cargo were established differently than before. During the earlier period the rates were supposedly set to cover operators' fully allocated costs, meaning not only the incremental costs of carrying a particular shipment, but a proportionate share of operators' overhead costs also. But were operators' costs measured net of operating differential subsidy, in the case of carriers receiving such subsidy, or gross of subsidy? Or to ask the question another way, were freight rates intended to be remunerative to unsubsidized as well as subsidized lines?

The answer to the last question almost certainly is yes, although by 1966, after a decade and a half of constantly increasing costs, followed by regular increases in rates, it could no longer have been clear to anyone what relation military freight rates bore to operators' costs. But apparently it was common opinion that military freight rates actually covered costs before payment of the operating subsidy. Evidently the unsubsidized lines thought so; for during this period they expressed no complaints that rates were too low because the rates reflected the costs of subsidized lines after receipt of subsidy, in contrast to their complaints in the late 1960s that subsidized lines were able to underbid unsubsidized operators because a part of the former's costs was paid by the operating subsidy.

Some corroborative evidence appeared early in 1971 among material submitted to the Maritime Subsidy Board during a hearing to decide whether the operating differential subsidy should continue to be paid for voyages on which the cargoes being carried were largely preference cargoes. A study was made of the costs and revenues of subsidized lines in 1964, 1966, 1968, and 1969. The operators' total costs were allocated among classes of cargo in proportion to the space that each shipment occupied. The study found that in both 1964 and 1966, for all lines together, the revenue received for the carriage of military cargo more than covered the costs allocable to such cargo *before* payment of subsidy. In contrast, the cost of carrying commercial nonpreference cargo greatly exceeded revenues from such cargo.[5]

It may therefore be supposed that at least until 1966, freight rates for the carriage of military cargo were set to cover gross operating costs of

5. American Maritime Association, *Cargo Revenue and Expense of Subsidized Carriers by Cargo Category*, Exhibit N-4 (revised) submitted to the Maritime Subsidy Board, Maritime Administration, Docket S-244 (1971; processed), hereafter referred to as AMA, Maritime Subsidy Board Docket S-244, exhibit N-4 (revised).

U.S. flag vessels. If one assumes that foreign rates would have roughly reflected foreign costs, the difference in rates between foreign and U.S. carriers would have been approximately equal to the difference in costs. The reasoning is parallel to that supporting the estimates in chapter 5 of the costs of the cabotage laws.

How large were the differences throughout this period between the operating costs of U.S. flag and foreign flag vessels? No exact answer can be given. Not only are comprehensive cost figures lacking, but one may be sure that if they were available they would be highly variable, depending on the identity of the U.S. and foreign lines, the routes on which the lines were competing, the vessels the lines were operating, and so forth. Still, some information is available. According to figures from the Maritime Administration, the vessel operating expenses of subsidized U.S. flag liners have for a number of years been somewhat more than twice as great as the corresponding expenses of their foreign competitors.[6] Accordingly, I might conservatively estimate that between 1952 and 1966 the cost of shipping military cargoes on U.S. liners was twice as great as it would have been if the Military Sealift Command had moved its cargoes on foreign flag liners.[7]

Much the same approach may be used in connection with vessels chartered by the command. If one assumes that charter rates for U.S. flag tankers and dry cargo vessels were also roughly twice as high during much of this period as the rates for foreign flag vessels, the extra cost of shipping military cargoes aboard U.S. flag vessels, including both vessels in berth service and vessels chartered by the command, must have exceeded $100 million each fiscal year between 1952 and 1966. For all fifteen years, the extra cost totaled more than $2 billion.

It is more difficult to estimate a similar cost for the years after 1966. In the first place, it is not clear whether military freight rates reflected vessel operating costs before subsidy or after subsidy. Beginning in 1967

6. No figures are available before 1960. In that year vessel operating expenses of subsidized operators were 1.9 times as great as those of their foreign competitors. In both 1965 and 1969 the figure was 2.1. (Information furnished by U.S. Maritime Administration, Office of Subsidy Administration.) For sake of simplicity, I shall say that U.S. expenses were twice as great as foreign expenses throughout this period, recognizing that in the 1950s the correct multiple may have been slightly lower.

7. This estimate may be somewhat high. Lawrence concluded in 1966 that U.S. flag rates were probably no more than 40 percent to 50 percent higher than foreign flag rates between 1954 and 1964. Samuel A. Lawrence, *United States Merchant Shipping Policies and Politics* (Brookings Institution, 1966), p. 208.

most military shipments carried by liners moved at rates established by a procedure similar to competitive bidding. (Hereafter I shall ignore the difference and speak of competitive rate making.) At ordinary levels of demand, one would have expected subsidized lines to consistently under-bid unsubsidized lines for military cargoes, assuming that operating costs for the two groups of carriers were approximately the same. The receipt of subsidies equal in aggregate to about one-half of vessel operating expenses in 1969 should have given subsidized carriers an insurmountable competitive advantage over unsubsidized lines. And so it did, according to the unsubsidized lines, which complained bitterly over the "double subsidy"[8] their rivals were receiving, and which in 1969 brought action before the Maritime Subsidy Board to force the Maritime Administration to withhold operating subsidies from contractors in proportion to the volume of preference cargo that they carried.

The same financial data from the double subsidy hearing that were cited above disclose that in both 1968 and 1969 the revenues that subsidized lines received for the carriage of military cargoes either covered or nearly covered a proportionate share of the lines' total expenses *before* receipt of subsidy.[9] The unsubsidized lines interpreted these data as proving that military freight rates were truly premium freight rates that covered U.S. costs before subsidy, and they claimed that the subsidized lines were therefore unfairly receiving a double subsidy. Without committing oneself to the legal implications that the unsubsidized lines drew out of these data —that the subsidized lines should therefore return a portion of the operating subsidies they had been paid—one may observe that freight rates for military cargo certainly remained high compared with freight rates for other classes of cargo, despite the introduction of competitive rate making. The reason seems clear. In the middle 1960s, exports of military cargoes suddenly soared when the United States began to build up its forces in

8. The term "double subsidy" refers to the twin benefits that subsidized lines allegedly receive whenever they carry preference cargo. One benefit is given in the form of operating differential subsidies, which the lines receive no matter what kind of cargo they carry. The other benefit is contained in the higher rates they are paid for the carriage of preference cargo.

9. AMA, Maritime Subsidy Board Docket S-244, exhibit N-4 (revised). A proportionate share means an operator's total expenses multiplied by the ratio of the space occupied by military cargo to the space occupied by all cargo. If every class of cargo earned revenue in amounts that more than covered a proportionate share of total expenses before subsidy, the lines would need no operating differential subsidies at all, because they would earn a profit without them.

Vietnam. Military shipments to destinations overseas more than doubled, from 3.4 million long tons in 1964 to 7.6 million long tons in 1967.[10] This explosion of demand for shipping space coincided with the introduction of competitive rate making, and must explain why freight rates remained high. Carriers could continue to charge their customary rates for military shipments, knowing very well that there was ample cargo for all lines whatever rates they asked, subject only to the constraint in the cargo preference laws that the rates should not exceed those paid by commercial shippers. In short, competitive rate making had no chance to lower military freight rates until demand for shipping space abated.

Military shipments did fall after 1967: to 6.6 million long tons in 1968 and 6.2 million long tons in 1969.[11] Assuming that the supply of shipping space changed very little, it may be expected that this decline should have led to a fall in military freight rates. The MSC keeps no record of freight rates, so it is impossible to test this assumption directly. But the same data cited above disclose that between 1968 and 1969 the ratio of the revenue from military shipments to the fully allocated costs of their carriage did decline slightly on ten of the eleven steamship routes on which a sizable volume of military cargo moved both years; and on the eleventh route the ratio did not increase.[12] The declines were in most cases small; it is, however, not their size but their consistency that is significant.

The difficulty in developing trustworthy estimates of the cost of using only U.S. flag vessels for the carriage of military cargoes after 1966 should now be apparent. If the price of shipping space had fallen to the level of U.S. costs *net* of subsidy after competitive rate making had been established, as I expect it would have done if demand had not increased greatly, U.S. flag vessels would have been no more costly to use than foreign flag vessels, assuming that U.S. costs after subsidy were no higher than foreign costs. The increase in demand kept military freight rates from falling, and for several years after 1966 they apparently remained at levels that covered U.S. costs before subsidy.

---

10. American Institute of Merchant Shipping, *The Impact of Government-Impelled Cargo on the United States Merchant Marine*, vol. 2, Exhibits submitted to the Maritime Subsidy Board, Maritime Administration, Docket S-244 (1970; processed), exhibit 1. This volume is hereinafter referred to as AIMS, Maritime Subsidy Board Docket S-244.

11. Ibid.

12. AMA, Maritime Subsidy Board Docket S-244, exhibit N-4 (revised). A sizable volume means military cargo movements that generated at least $1 million of freight revenue each year.

The question now to be considered is how much the price of shipping would have fallen if foreign flag vessels were permitted to compete for military cargoes. I answered this question for the period before 1966 by stating that the price would have fallen to the level of foreign costs. It is not at all clear that the same answer is warranted for the period after 1966. The extraordinary surge of demand for shipping space by the Military Sealift Command in 1966 and 1967 surely would have strained even available foreign flag capacity, had foreign vessels been eligible carriers. In aggregate, foreign flag vessels leave U.S. ports with more dry cargo than they bring,[13] so it is fair to presume that ordinarily they have little vacant outbound space.

To be sure, even in 1967 the volume of military shipments bound overseas from the United States, although large, was still very much smaller than the volume of outbound commercial cargoes that foreign lines carried. Between 1966 and 1967, when outbound military shipments increased most rapidly, the increase from one year to the next in the amount of military tonnage carried aboard liners amounted to slightly less than six percent of the volume of outbound commercial cargoes aboard all foreign liners in 1967.[14] But the increase must have been concentrated on just a few routes, above all on the Pacific coast–Far East trade route. In order to accommodate this traffic, foreign lines would have had to greatly augment their regular sailings. Liners would have been forced to leave other routes. Under such circumstances, freight rates might not have fallen as low as they would in periods of less frantic demand.

In conclusion, although no one can be certain at what price the Military Sealift Command might have procured space aboard foreign flag liners during the Vietnam War, the price would surely have been much lower than American vessels were paid, though not as low as foreign costs. If one has to pick a figure, shipping costs might have been 40 percent lower in 1967, 1968, and 1969, instead of 50 percent lower as I assumed for the period before.

By the end of the 1960s, the demand for space to Vietnam had greatly diminished. Competition among U.S. lines for break-bulk cargoes intensified, and unsubsidized lines complained that the subsidized carriers were constantly underbidding them. This was to be expected. As fewer cargoes became available more spirited bidding should have followed and rates

13. U.S. Bureau of the Census, *Statistical Abstract of the United States: 1974* (1974), table 984, p. 584.
14. AIMS, Maritime Subsidy Board Docket S-244, exhibit 1.

should have fallen. If the competition of subsidized lines forced rates down to the level of carriers' costs *after* subsidy, those rates would not be much higher than the rates we expect foreign lines would charge. Unfortunately there are no data whatever relating operators' revenues to operators' costs for the years after 1969. I would hazard a guess that military freight rates might have been 30 percent lower in fiscal 1970 if foreign flag vessels had competed for cargoes, 20 percent lower in fiscal 1971, and 15 percent lower in fiscal 1972.

The Military Sealift Command also chartered a sizable quantity of U.S. flag tonnage to meet its shipping requirements during the second half of the 1960s. The new procedure for establishing freight rates that the command instituted in 1966 affected only the rates that it paid for space aboard liners, not those that it paid for chartering vessels. Hence I can assume as before that charter rates for U.S. vessels remained roughly twice as high as the rates for foreign vessels. This estimate, like others above, is conservative. At times during the past several years foreign charter rates have apparently been as low as 40 percent of U.S. rates.

During the first eleven months of 1967 just 11.1 percent by tonnage of MSC shipments aboard liners moved in containers. Two years later, for the period between October 1, 1968, and September 30, 1969, the fraction had risen to 42.5 percent.[15] By mid-1974 it must be well over one-half. This rapid increase in the use of containers by the Military Sealift Command greatly complicates the task of estimating the cost of the cargo preference laws. Containerized shipping was pioneered by a few U.S. steamship lines, notably by Sea-Land Service, Inc., and for a few years this highly productive innovation enabled them to compete effectively with foreign break-bulk carriers for commercial cargoes. Many foreign lines are also currently offering containerized shipping services, and U.S. lines no longer enjoy the advantage they did. But for a time late in the 1960s, when the MSC began shipping in containers in volume, U.S. carriers were the only ones offering this service. Therefore if the command intended to use containers at all, it had to patronize U.S. lines, and it would be erroneous to ascribe the command's custom solely to the requirements of the cargo preference laws.

Until 1972 the Military Sealift Command made no distinction in its financial reports between payments for the movement of containers and payments for the movement of break-bulk cargoes. Accordingly, I have

15. Ibid., exhibit 59.

had to improvise my own estimates of the way payments were divided between these classes. I assume that the following fractions of the payments the command made under shipping agreements in each fiscal year beginning in 1967 were made for containerized services: 1967, 10 percent; 1968, 20 percent; 1969, 30 percent; 1970, 40 percent; 1971 and after, 50 percent. I assume that the shipping services these payments bought could not have been obtained more cheaply from foreign lines. And so it is only the remaining payments that I multiply by the factors I chose earlier to obtain estimates of the cost for which the same shipping services could have been got from foreign carriers.

An example may help clarify this procedure. In fiscal year 1968 the Military Sealift Command paid $317.7 million for space aboard liners.[16] I estimate that 20 percent of these payments were made for the carriage of containers. The balance of $254 million was paid for break-bulk shipments. I further estimate that the containerized service could not have been bought more cheaply from foreign flag lines, if indeed such lines could have provided it at all, but that the space that was purchased with the remaining $254 million could have been obtained from foreign carriers at a saving of 40 percent—about $100 million.

That same year the command spent $480.3 million for chartered shipping. I assume the command could have obtained the same quantity of foreign flag shipping for half the price, at a saving of about $240 million.

Adding these figures, I obtain an estimate of $340 million as the extra cost to the Military Sealift Command in 1968 of transporting military supplies in U.S. flag vessels only. Similar estimates for other fiscal years appear in the text (see Table 7-4, p. 89). They show that between 1952 and 1972 the MSC was forced to spend an additional $3.8 billion to satisfy the requirement that all military supplies moving overseas must be carried in U.S. flag vessels. This estimate is obviously imprecise; but whatever the true cost was—and it may have been as little as $3 billion or as much as $5 billion—it has definitely been sizable in comparison with the costs of other federal maritime aids.

Only the additional costs attributable to the command's use of *privately owned* U.S. flag vessels have been considered here. Nothing has been included for the use of vessels of the command's nucleus fleet. The decision to exclude the latter vessels is admittedly arbitrary. Perhaps in the absence

16. The sum of the figures that appear in the command's accounts under the headings of shipping agreements, shipping contracts, and berth terms (Military Sealift Command, *Financial and Statistical Report,* pts. 1 and 2).

of the cargo preference laws the Defense Department would maintain a smaller nucleus fleet and rely more heavily on cheaper foreign flag shipping than it relies today on privately owned U.S. flag shipping. Or perhaps it would prefer to make less use of all private shipping, whatever the flag, and would increase the size of the nucleus fleet. Arguments could be offered in support of either assumption, or in support of a third assumption that the size of the nucleus fleet is determined principally by strategic considerations and would not be affected by repeal of the cargo preference laws. But this is too speculative an issue for me to venture any answer here, and so I offer only these more limited cost estimates.

Bibliography

Arthur D. Little, Inc. "Ship Construction Differential Subsidies." Report to the Maritime Administration, U.S. Department of Commerce. Processed, 1961.

Barker, James R., and Robert Brandwein. *The United States Merchant Marine in National Perspective.* Lexington, Mass.: Heath Lexington Books, 1970.

Bennathan, Esra, and A. A. Walters. *The Economics of Ocean Freight Rates.* New York: Frederick A. Praeger, 1969.

Clark, Earl W., Hoyt S. Haddock, and Stanley J. Volens. *The U.S. Merchant Marine Today: Sunrise or Sunset?* Washington: Labor-Management Maritime Committee, 1970.

Committee of Inquiry into Shipping. *Report.* Cmnd. 4337. London: Her Majesty's Stationery Office, 1970.

Ferguson, Allen R., and others. *The Economic Value of the United States Merchant Marine.* Evanston, Ill.: The Transportation Center at Northwestern University, 1961.

Gorter, Wytze. *United States Shipping Policy.* New York: Harper and Brothers, for the Council on Foreign Relations, 1956.

Goss, R. O. *Studies in Maritime Economics.* Cambridge: Cambridge University Press, 1968.

Grossman, William L. *Ocean Freight Rates.* Cambridge, Md.: Cornell Maritime Press, 1956.

Harbridge House. "The Balance of Payments and the U.S. Merchant Marine." Processed. Boston: Harbridge House, Inc., 1968. Reprinted in Barker and Brandwein, *The United States Merchant Marine in National Perspective,* Appendix C.

Hutchins, John G. B. *The American Maritime Industries and Public Policy, 1789–1914: An Economic History.* Cambridge: Harvard University Press, 1941; New York: Russell & Russell, 1969.

Larner, Robert. "Public Policy in the Ocean Freight Industry," in Almarin Phillips, ed., *Promoting Competition in Regulated Markets.* Washington: Brookings Institution, 1975.

Lawrence, Samuel A. *United States Merchant Shipping Policies and Politics.* Washington: Brookings Institution, 1966.

McDowell, Carl E., and Helen M. Gibbs. *Ocean Transportation.* New York: McGraw-Hill Book Company, 1954.

Madigan, Richard E. *Taxation of the Shipping Industry.* Cambridge, Md.: Cornell Maritime Press, 1971.

Metaxas, B. N. *The Economics of Tramp Shipping.* London: The Athlone Press, 1971.

Moyer, R. Charles, and Harold Handerson. "A Critique of the Rationales
for Present U.S. Maritime Programs," *Transportation Journal,* Vol. 14
(Winter 1974).

National Academy of Sciences–National Research Council. Maritime Research Advisory Committee. *The Role of the U. S. Merchant Marine in National Security.* Project WALRUS Report by the Panel on Wartime Use of
the U.S. Merchant Marine. Publication 748. Washington: National Academy of Sciences–National Research Council, 1959.

O'Loughlin, Carleen. *The Economics of Sea Transport.* Oxford: Pergamon
Press, 1967.

Reese, Howard C., ed. *Merchant Marine Policy.* Proceedings of the Sym-
posium of the Fifteenth Ocean Shipping Management Institute of the American University's School of Business Administration. Cambridge, Md.:
Cornell Maritime Press, 1963.

Richardson, David M. "Capital Construction Funds under the Merchant
Marine Act," *Tax Law Review,* Vol. 29 (Summer 1974).

U.S. Congress. House of Representatives. *Scope and Effect of Tax Benefits
Provided in the Maritime Industry.* A Report by the Secretary of the Treasury. House Document 213. 82 Cong. 1 sess. Washington: Government
Printing Office, 1951. Reprinted in *Long-Range Shipping Bill,* Hearings
before the House Committee on Merchant Marine and Fisheries, 82 Cong.
2 sess. (1952), pp. 45–67.

U.S. Congress. House of Representatives. Committee on Merchant Marine
and Fisheries. Subcommittee on Merchant Marine. *Cargo for American
Ships.* Hearings. Part 1: 92 Cong. 1 sess. Part 2: 92 Cong. 2 sess. Washington:
Government Printing Office, 1972.

U.S. Congress. House of Representatives. Committee on Merchant Marine
and Fisheries. Subcommittee on Merchant Marine. *Energy Transportation
Security Act of 1974.* Hearings. 93 Cong. 1 and 2 sess. Washington:
Government Printing Office, 1974.

U.S. Congress. House of Representatives. Committee on Merchant Marine
and Fisheries. Subcommittee on Merchant Marine. *Independent Federal
Maritime Administration.* Hearings. 90 Cong. 1 sess. Washington: Government Printing Office, 1967.

U.S. Congress. House of Representatives. Committee on Merchant Marine
and Fisheries. Subcommittee on Merchant Marine. *Long-Range Maritime
Program.* Hearings. 90 Cong. 2 sess. Washington: Government Printing
Office, 1968.

U.S. Congress. House of Representatives. Committee on Merchant Marine
and Fisheries. Subcommittee on Merchant Marine. *President's Maritime
Program.* Hearings. Part 1: 91 Cong. 1 sess. Part 2: 91 Cong. 2 sess. Washington: Government Printing Office, 1970.

U.S. Congress. House of Representatives. Subcommittee on Merchant Marine
and the Committee on Merchant Marine and Fisheries. *Passenger Vessels.*
Hearings. 92 Cong. 1 sess. Washington: Government Printing Office, 1971.

U.S. Congress. Senate. *Discriminatory Ocean Freight Rates and the Balance of*

Payments. Report No. 1. 89 Cong. 1 sess. Washington: Government Printing Office, 1965.

U.S. Congress. Senate. Committee on Commerce. Subcommittee on Merchant Marine. *Energy Transportation Security Act of 1974.* Hearings. 93 Cong. 2 sess. Washington: Government Printing Office, 1974.

U.S. Congress. Senate. Committee on Commerce. Subcommittee on Merchant Marine. *The Maritime Program.* Hearings. 91 Cong. 2 sess. Washington: Government Printing Office, 1970.

U.S. Department of Commerce. "Maritime Resources for Security and Trade." Final Report of the Maritime Evaluation Committee to the Secretary of Commerce. Washington: U.S. Department of Commerce. Processed 1963.

U.S. Department of Commerce. Maritime Administration. *Maritime Subsidies.* Washington: Government Printing Office, 1974.

U.S. Department of Commerce. Maritime Administration. Office of Policy and Plans. *U.S. Passenger Ship Fleet: Summary and Prospects.* U.S. Department of Commerce, Maritime Administration, 1973.

U.S. Department of Defense. "Sealift Procurement and National Security (SPANS) Study." Prepared at the direction of the Deputy Secretary of Defense. Part I: "Understanding the Current Systems." Part II: "The Future Size, Composition, and Productivity of the U.S. Merchant Marine and Forecasts of U.S. Waterborne Trade." Part III: "Defense Implications." Part IV: "Alternative Procurement Systems." Processed. 1972.

S. Interagency Maritime Task Force. "The Merchant Marine in National Defense and Trade: A Policy and a Program." Processed. 1965.

S. Maritime Advisory Committee. "Maritime Policy and Program of the United States." Report and Recommendations of the Public Members of the Maritime Advisory Committee, submitted to the Full Committee for its Consideration [and adopted by a majority vote of the committee membership, with dissents by H. Lee White and others]. Processed. 1965. Reprinted in *Vietnam—Shipping Policy Review,* Hearings before the Subcommittee on Merchant Marine of the House Committee on Merchant Marine and Fisheries, 89 Cong. 2 sess. (1966), Part 1, pp. 140–90.

U.S. Maritime Commission. *Economic Survey of the American Merchant Marine.* Washington: Government Printing Office, 1937.

Zeis, Paul Maxwell. *American Shipping Policy.* Princeton: Princeton University Press, 1938.

U.
  I
U

i.

Social Responsibility and the Business Predicament

JAMES W. McKIE, Editor

Business as we know it, emerging in Western Europe several centuries ago, developed a set of organizations, functions, purposes, and methods separate from other social institutions long before it defined a creed of its own. After a time Adam Smith's classical model prevailed, according to which businessmen seeking profits in a competitive market automatically serve the public good by serving their own interest. This model, however, always somewhat remote from everyday reality, had to be altered eventually to accommodate additional economic and social concerns such as income distribution, price stability, and employment. More recently, the so-called managerial model has become prominent. Corporation managers see themselves as trustees of permanent institutions that recognize obligations not only to proprietors but also to employees, customers, suppliers, and the community. Some advocates of this view would say that the self-interest of a corporation is tightly linked with the well-being of the entire society of which it is part. On the other hand, radical critics of business argue that the corporations thrive by creating artificial wants and encouraging the production of unnecessary goods to satisfy them.

Thus the question of business responsibility remains controversial, just as it was in the seventeenth century. A group of economists and public affairs analysts assembled by Brookings applied their knowledge and insight to the issue with the results presented in this volume, the eleventh in the Brookings series of Studies in the Regulation of Economic Activity:

• Two chapters deal with the internal organization of business—Marvin Chirelstein writing on the law of incorporation and Thomas C. Schelling on command and control within the firm.

• Two chapters cover relations between business and government—Roland McKean on the mechanisms available to government to promote business responsibility and James Q. Wilson on the politics of business regulation.

• As constituents of business, the consumer and the employee are discussed—by Martin Bronfenbrenner and Charles A. Myers, respectively.

• The impact of business on the environment is examined by Jerome Rothenberg, and responsibility in special locales is the subject of three chapters—John Kain on business and the city, Benjamin Chinitz on depressed areas, and Raymond Vernon on foreign operations.

• The editor of the book provides a general introduction.

James W. McKie, a member of the Brookings associated staff, is dean of the School of Social and Behavioral Sciences at the University of Texas.

361pp/1975/paper and cloth

Studies in the Regulation of Economic Activity

THE BROOKINGS INSTITUTION / WASHINGTON, D.C.

ISBN 0-8157-4574-5

Index

Africa, 71, 72
Agency for International Development (AID), 75, 77; administration of foreign aid commodity shipments, 94, 96, 97
Agricultural Act of *1956*, 95n
Agricultural commodities: barter program for, 90; in Food for Peace Program, 89, 90; value of exported, 108
Agricultural Trade Development and Assistance Act of *1954*. *See* Public Law 480
AID. *See* Agency for International Development
Alaska, 46, 59, 60
Argentina, S.S., 32
Australia, 72

Balance of payments: exchange rates and, 111–14; foreign exchange earnings and savings and, 104–06; impact of merchant marine on, 99, 106–09, 115, 134
Balance of payments benefit: explanation of, 109; from merchant shipping operations, 110–11, 117, 141; from subsidies to shipbuilding industry, 114–15
Barker, James R., 99n, 109
Barter program. *See* Public Law 480
Bilateral agreements, on cargo transport, 12–13
Boczek, Boleslaw Adam, 3n
Boyd, Alan S., 41n
Brandwein, Robert, 99n, 109
Brasil, S.S., 32
Brazil, 93n
Brooklyn, T.T., 132n
Bulk carriers: commodities carried by, 27; construction subsidies for, 42; in effective U.S. control fleet, 130; operating subsidies for, 24–25, 27, 29; preference cargoes shipped by, 27n, 72–73; role in military operations, 125. *See also* Dry cargo vessels; Tankers

Cabotage: costs of, 45, 49–53, 139; explanation of, 45
Cabotage laws, 3n, 11, 14, 46–48
Calkins, Robert D., 6, 7
Canada, 3n
Capital construction funds: accounts in, 58; administration of, 60; establishment of, 55; penalties for nonqualified withdrawals from, 60; use of, 59, 60
Capital gains, tax-deferred deposits of, 57, 66, 68
Capital reserve funds. *See* Capital construction funds
Cargoes: bilateral agreements for, 12–13; bulk, 24–25, 26, 27, 29; competition for, 77; containerized, 72, 73; dry bulk, 26, 27n, 29, 84, 86; foreign assistance, 89–96; government, 69, 81; "government-impelled," 12, 140; grain, 12n, 27, 31n; liner, 26, 27, 29, 95, 96, 97; measurement of, 84–85; petroleum, 26, 29, 86, 87; tanker, 26, 72, 97; third-country carriage of, 12, 13; tramp, 72, 95, 96, 97; weight versus value of, 28–29. *See also* Military cargo; Preference cargo
Cargo preference. *See* Preference cargo
Cargo Preference Act of *1954*, 79–80; AID shipments under, 96; Public Law 480 shipments under, 91, 94; requirements for military cargo, 84; World Food Program shipments under, 96n
Cargo preference laws: cost of, 73–77, 80–81, 88, 91, 93, 94, 95, 96, 98, 140; explanation of, 11–12, 69; fiscal and nonfiscal characteristics of, 13; as indirect subsidy, 73; provisions of, 78–80; waiver from, 79, 80. *See also* Cargo Preference Act of *1954*; Military Transportation Act of *1904*; Public Resolution No. 17 of *1934*.
Charter vessels, 24, 83, 84, 85, 87, 88. *See also* Bulk carriers

159